The Complete Guide to Becoming a

Successful Mortgage Broker

Insider Secrets You Need to Know

By Patricia Hughes

THE COMPLETE GUIDE TO BECOMING A SUCCESSFUL MORTGAGE BROKER: INSIDER SECRETS YOU NEED TO KNOW

1405 SW 6th Ave. • Ocala, Florida 34471 • 352-622-1825 • 352-622-1875–Fax
Web site: www.atlantic-pub.com • E-mail: sales@atlantic-pub.com
SAN Number: 268-1250

ISBN-13: 978-1-60138-257-3 ISBN-10: 1-60138-257-X

Library of Congress Cataloging-in-Publication Data

Hughes, Patricia, 1968-
The complete guide to becoming a successful mortgage broker : insider secrets you need to know / by Patricia Hughes.
p. cm.
Includes bibliographical references and index.
ISBN-13: 978-1-60138-130-9 (alk. paper)
ISBN-10: 1-60138-130-1 (alk. paper)
1. Mortgage brokers--United States. I. Title.

HG2040.5.U5H845 2008
332.7'202373--dc22
2008024607

INTERIOR LAYOUT DESIGN: Vickie Taylor • vtaylor@atlantic-pub.com

Printed in the United States

Dedication

To my children

Table of Contents

For Sale

CHAPTER

1

Getting Started

What Is a Mortgage Broker?

The best place to start a discussion about becoming a successful mortgage broker is with a definition. A mortgage broker is a financial professional who acts as an agent between borrowers looking for mortgages and the institutions that offer them. The term mortgage broker is used to refer to both the individual broker and the brokerage firm.

It is the job of the mortgage broker to find a lender that offers a program that best suits the needs of the borrower. A mortgage broker works with a number of lenders, with the range being as low as 10 or as high as 100, depending on the mortgage broker. The large number of lenders allows the broker to find more loans than a borrower ever could on his own.

The mortgage broker contracts with the borrower and takes the application. The mortgage broker then presents the loan to several lenders with programs that fit the borrower's needs. The borrower could do this without a mortgage broker, but it is time consuming, and the broker has access to better rates than those offered directly to home buyers.

The mortgage broker offers another valuable benefit to the borrower. He makes a recommendation on the best loan option, based on his expertise and the borrower's financial situation. Comparing rates, terms, points, and conditions are difficult without knowledge and experience. This is what the mortgage broker offers to the borrower.

According to the National Association of Realtors, 65 percent of borrowers use a mortgage broker to secure a home loan. As consumers realize the benefits of using a broker, the demand will continue to increase. This is good news for professional mortgage brokers and those entering the field.

The bulk of the mortgage broker's day is spent on two main tasks: finding clients and finding loans for existing clients. New brokers are often surprised at the amount of time that needs to be devoted to finding borrowers. The job of finding new clients is important and not just in the beginning of your career. New business is needed on a continual basis to earn commission, which is how brokers are paid.

How to Get Started in Business

There are no specific educational requirements to become a mortgage broker. No colleges or universities offer a degree program specifically for mortgage brokers. Some states require a class be taken prior to the certification exam, but a college degree is not required. Some brokers do have a business or finance degree, but others do not.

The benefit of having the degree is mainly for public relations purposes. Clients tend to have more confidence in a professional with a degree, which is a hurdle for new mortgage brokers. Once the broker has established himself in the community and has relationships with mortgage lenders, the degree becomes less important. The broker is able to focus on his success and business reputation to acquire new clients, even without a diploma hanging on the wall.

Professionals with a college degree tend to earn more money, particularly when they are working for a brokerage firm. With a graduate degree, the earning potential is even higher. Mortgage brokers with a master's in business administration or a master's in finance can earn 15 to 20 percent more than a broker with a bachelor's degree or no degree at all. Some larger companies offer tuition reimbursement that allows brokers to return to school at the company's expense.

Formal education is a plus, but more is needed to become a successful mortgage broker. There are certain skills that are needed in this industry that cannot be learned in college. An effective mortgage broker needs to have good people skills, be good at reading people, have the ability to think on his feet, and make adjustments based on the situation.

A good broker also needs sales and marketing skills. When a mortgage broker is searching for clients, he is selling himself. Professionals with previous sales and marketing experience often have the skills needed to succeed as a mortgage broker and tend to do well in this field.

The mortgage broker industry is regulated on both the state and federal levels. The professional broker must meet the requirements and follow all laws related to the industry. Licensing fees, background investigations, surety bonds, and mortgage classes may be required, depending on the state in which the broker will be licensed.

Developing Relationships With Lenders

One of the most important components of getting started in the mortgage broker business is developing relationships with lenders. To become successful and offer the best possible service to borrowers, the mortgage broker must work with many mortgage lenders. If the mortgage broker has good relationships with underwriters and processors that work for the lenders, his job can be much easier.

The lender/mortgage broker relationship is mutually beneficial. The mortgage broker gets paid when loans close. The more loans that close, the more money the broker makes. To close more loans, the broker needs lenders. The more lenders the mortgage broker can cultivate relationships with, the more programs and choices he is able to offer his clients.

The lenders benefit from the relationship as well, as they have a product to sell. To attract borrowers, the lender spends a lot of money on advertising. A broker makes the job of the lender much easier. He brings borrowers to the lender. Since the mortgage broker spent his own money to find his client, the lender has saved both time and money.

This relationship is so profitable that mortgage lenders have departments dedicated to working directly with mortgage brokers. This department offers mortgages at wholesale rates that offer better deals than customers get when they contact the lender directly. This results in a lower interest rate for the borrower.

There are two basic ways to get started in the mortgage broker business. You can work for a company or start your own firm. There are benefits and drawbacks to both options. These will be covered in the next section. Learn about each and weigh the pros and cons to make the best choice for your personal career success as a mortgage broker.

Working for a Company

The vast majority of mortgage brokers start out their careers working for a company. Working for a company has benefits for the new mortgage broker. One of the biggest benefits of working for a company is the on-the-job training available. New brokers are often paired with a more experienced broker, especially in larger firms. The experienced broker acts as a mentor, helping the new mortgage broker navigate the business and learn the ropes.

There is other training available on an ongoing basis with a large brokerage firm. Take advantage of all training offered by the company. The knowledge gained is valuable for achieving success as a mortgage broker. These training classes and workshops can be used to meet the continuing-education requirement for license renewal. The company will track your hours and courses taken, which saves even more time.

State requirements may dictate your decision to work for a company. Some state regulations require a minimum number of years' experience before a mortgage broker is able to open his own firm. This experience can be obtained by working for a company. Other states require that an applicant be sponsored by a company to be granted a license. In this case, the broker would need to be hired and then take the licensing exam.

Choosing a Company

If you have decided to work for a company, choose carefully. All mortgage broker companies are not created equal. The working conditions and pay scale vary widely between large and small companies. Pay can be either straight commission or a combination of a smaller base salary and smaller commission on each loan that is closed.

The support at all companies is not equal either. Some offer more support to new mortgage brokers than others. The amount of support available at the company is an important consideration when making an employment decision. To the new broker looking to gain valuable experience, this may be even more important than the payment structure, provided the salary opportunity is sufficient as well.

The size of the company is another consideration when looking for a job. There are benefits to both large and small companies. Larger firms tend to offer more support and training opportunities than smaller firms. There is a wider range of training courses offered in companies that employ a large number of brokers. Larger companies also have more resources and can afford to offer a wider selection of training classes. At a large firm, the broker may never need to go anywhere else to get Continuing Education Units (CEUs) for license renewal.

There are negative aspects to working for a large brokerage firm. The biggest negative aspect is the competitiveness in some large firms. The competition can get rather cutthroat with so many mortgage brokers going after the same leads. In some firms, the quotas and incentive systems feed into the competitiveness and help propagate the cutthroat tactics of the brokers employed by the company.

Small companies also offer opportunities to the new broker. In a small firm, the new mortgage broker has the opportunity to learn more aspects of the mortgage business. There are fewer employees doing the work, and the broker may take on more responsibilities and learn more as a result. This is especially beneficial for new brokers who intend to open their own businesses.

Because there are fewer people employed at a smaller firm, the brokers who work there have the chance to make more of a contribution. The mortgage brokers can have an impact on policy and their suggestions may be taken into consideration more than at a large company with more-established procedures. In an atmosphere with less competition, the broker also has a greater chance to stand out and make an impression than in a firm with many brokers all grappling for the spotlight.

The biggest negative issue with working for a smaller company is that the mortgage broker works harder. The broker often is called upon to do more than his job. At times, this can be a hardship as it cuts into the time the mortgage broker spends attracting new business and servicing clients.

Do not jump at the first job offer. Choose a company with a solid reputation in the community. The reputation of the firm will help you build your reputation as a mortgage professional. If the company has a good reputation, this can help your authority with potential clients. The opposite can also be true. A company with a poor reputation can damage the reputation of the new broker.

Working for Yourself

The income potential is higher when a mortgage broker is self-employed. The standard practice is a 50/50 split between the broker and the firm that employs the broker. When the broker is self-employed, he keeps all the commission earned on a loan. The broker could actually close half the number of loans and still earn the same money he earned working for a firm. If he closes the same number of loans, he has doubled his income since he is not splitting the commission with an employer.

The freedom of being self-employed is a big reason many mortgage brokers open their own firms. Business ownership and the freedom to be self-employed is a big piece of the "American Dream." This freedom comes at a price, as the mortgage broker must be motivated to work hard. It can be a lot easier to procrastinate or get caught up in issues not related to business when working from home.

The biggest challenge to the new self-employed broker is building a reputation and finding clients. This is easier to do when working for an established company. Contacts can be made that are useful later when the mortgage broker breaks out on his own. For this reason, many new brokers go to work for a company initially.

Once the broker has made contacts with lenders and other professionals and established a reputation as a successful broker, he is better prepared to start a business. The contacts made in the real estate and mortgage industry can then be used to build a client base for the newly established firm.

There is a way to have the best of both worlds. A mortgage broker working for a company may have the opportunity to telecommute, at least part of the time. The broker works from an office located in his home most of the time. He may be required to come into the office a few times each week for meetings or training.

If you decide to work from home, you will need the following:

- Computer with Internet access for e-mail communications
- Mortgage software that is compatible with software used in the office
- Telephone line with voice mail or an answering machine
- Fax machine
- Copy machine

Tax Advantages of a Home Office

Setting up a home office is not difficult or expensive, compared to other businesses. If you use a room in your house solely for business purposes, there can be significant tax advantages as well. The mortgage broker working from a home office can deduct a percentage of the mortgage, property taxes, and utility bills. The percentage depends on the square footage of the office and the overall square footage of the house.

To qualify for income tax purposes, certain conditions must be met. The home office must be used for work purposes only. This means the broker is not allowed to use the office as a guest room nor have an office in the family room. It must be a separate room used only as an office for business purposes.

When a mortgage broker is employed by a company and works from home most of the time, it must be at the convenience of the employer to claim a home office deduction on income tax returns. Fortunately, this is not difficult in the mortgage broker industry. Many employers prefer their brokers work from home, which saves the company money.

Speak with a tax accountant to determine what expenses can and cannot be deducted in your situation. When claiming business expenses, it is important to keep detailed records. Retain receipts for all equipment and supplies purchased throughout the year. Create a file for receipts or use an accordion file to organize and keep track of receipts. These can be found inexpensively at any office supply store. Good records are crucial since taxpayers who take the home office deduction are more likely to be audited.

CHAPTER 2

Licensing Requirements & Fees

The first step to becoming a mortgage broker is to get licensed. This is most likely a requirement in the state where you live. Even without the requirement, having a license is beneficial to the mortgage broker. It tells your clients that you are a professional in your field.

Licensing Requirements

Licensing requirements vary from state to state. Most states require some form of licensing or registration for mortgage brokers. Some require licensing only for the company and not for the individual broker. Others require that every broker working for the company be licensed.

A complete list of the requirements for each state, contact information, and fees can be found in the appendix at the back of this book. Refer to this listing for specific information about your state. Web sites are included for each state for easy reference.

There are benefits to obtaining a license even if the state does not require it for individuals. Having a license offers a degree of credibility to the broker, which is good for business. Customers like to see licenses and experience when they are choosing a broker to help secure a home loan. These customers are more likely to work with a broker who has a current license and has met all the state's requirements.

There is another good reason for brokers to obtain a license. After working for a company for a number of years, a broker may decide to open his own firm. At this point, a license will be required. If the broker has been licensed, he will not need to worry about meeting the requirements at that time, and the license will have been in effect for a number of years. This shows solid years of work experience in the mortgage industry. Without prior licensing, the broker will look like he has little or no experience prior to opening his firm.

Changes in Requirements

Requirements for a mortgage broker's license change frequently. Just a few years ago, Alaska and Colorado did not have any requirements or regulations for mortgage brokers. This is no longer the case. As of January 1, 2007, Colorado began requiring that brokers register with the state. Alaska will begin to require licensing for mortgage brokers on July 1, 2008.

Check with your state to determine if any recent changes have been made with regard to mortgage broker licensing. The Web sites and phone numbers are included in the listing of state requirements at the end of this book. This will help you determine if there have been any changes or if any are coming in the near future. Once you have your license, you may find that requirements change from one renewal period to the next, which is not unusual.

Required Coursework

Specific courses may be required for licensure, depending on the state in which a license is sought. Some have no requirements for either education or exams. Others require from one to three classes in addition to passing the required state mortgage broker exam. The benefit of these classes is that the material prepares students for the exam.

There are several options for completing the required coursework. Mortgage classes are offered at universities and community colleges. Some technical schools offer classes for mortgage brokers as well. Online courses are offered online through the National Association of Mortgage Brokers. The work for these classes can be done at home and e-mailed to the instructor or posted on a message board for the class. Courses are offered through mortgage broker's associations in each state in which the courses are required for licensing.

Exams and Fees

Passing an exam is required for mortgage broker licenses in many states. A variety of different exams are used, but each covers similar information. There will be common questions on all exams, regardless of the state issuing the license. Each area should be studied in detail prior to taking the exam. This preparation can be done in a class or at home, depending on the regulations of the state. This process can take a few months, since there is a lot of information to be covered.

Areas covered on licensing exams:

- Federal regulations
- State regulations
- Math calculations used in mortgage financing
- Real estate lending principles
- Laws regarding real estate
- State and federal laws on mortgage lending
- Basic knowledge about mortgage financing

Aspiring brokers need to take sufficient time to prepare for the exam. This is not something that can be studied for the night or even the week before. There is a large body of material covered on these tests and it takes time to learn it. In some states, courses are required prior to sitting for the state exam. In this case, the material on the exam will be covered in the class.

There is assistance available to prepare for the mortgage broker exams. Classes and workshops can be found in schools offering courses in the mortgage or real estate industries. Classes and workshops are offered online for most tests. Be sure the class has been developed for the specific exam used in your state before you use an online class for test preparation.

Exam prep study guides are sold for all exams. These can be found in college bookstores, some larger bookstores, and on the Internet. The study guide is a valuable resource for preparing for all types of certification exams. Information is included about the content of the test. Most have a practice test in the back of the book. Examinees can take the test after studying and determine which areas need more focus.

Tips for Preparing for the Exam

- Do not try to study all the material at once. Break it into smaller chunks and dedicate time to each section.
- Study a little bit each night for one to three months before the exam.
- If you are taking classes with others who will be taking the exam, pair up with a classmate for study sessions.
- Information can be put on index cards for easy reference and to study in free moments.
- Read notes and highlight pertinent information.
- Notes can be rewritten in outline form to make studying easier.
- Record notes on a cassette tape or burn a CD. Listen to the recording in the car, while preparing dinner, or working in the yard.
- Take the practice test in your study guide when you think you are ready.
- Go back and study the areas where improvement is needed after the practice test.

- Do not study the night before the exam. Eat a healthy dinner and get to bed early.

The licensing exam is a standardized test. There are some tried-and-true test-taking strategies that improve performance on standardized tests, whether it is the SAT exam for college, the GRE for graduate school, or the mortgage broker's exam. Utilize these strategies for the best possible score on the exam.

Test-Taking Tips

Listen carefully to all instructions prior to beginning the test. Read all directions completely before starting.

Read the entire question and all answer choices before selecting an answer. In some cases, they are looking for the best possible answer, and it can be easily missed if all answers are not read.

Read the wording of the question carefully. Simple words like "no" or "always" can significantly change the question.

Work in order and skip any questions that are difficult. Most tests are timed and time can run out quickly when excessive time is spent on certain questions. Skip the question and come back to it at the end.

When a question is skipped on the test, be sure to skip the corresponding line on the answer sheet to prevent big problems later.

If you still do not know the answer, take a guess. If there are four answer choices, you have a 25 percent chance of guessing the correct answer. If you can eliminate one or two of the answers, the chances of getting it right are even higher. When it is left blank, it is always wrong.

At least one answer can be eliminated from all test questions. Use the process of elimination to arrive at the correct answer if you are not sure.

Do not finish early. Take all the time allotted for the test. If there is time remaining, go back and check your answer sheet. Be sure all answers are filled in completely and there are no mistakes. Use this time to review difficult questions one more time.

Do not change your answers unless you are absolutely sure the answer is incorrect. Second guessing and changing answers is a bad test-taking strategy. Very often, the first answer is correct.

Look for clues in other questions. Valuable information may be found in the wording of other questions, especially with this type of exam. You may see something that will jog your memory.

In each state that requires an exam, there is a minimum score requirement to pass. If the applicant does not pass the exam on the first try, it can be taken again. Some states have a limit on how many times the test may be taken. Be aware of any limitations when planning to retake a test. If you do not pass the test on the first try, consider taking a class or workshop to help you prepare for the next test date.

The fees charged for licensing vary widely from state to state. In some states, the fee is as low as $250. In others, the fees can exceed $1,000. Fees are charged for mortgage classes, licensing, and exams. Most states fall in the $500 range for all fees related to licensing and background investigation.

Obtaining Additional Licenses

Once you have obtained a license in your home state, you may entertain the idea of applying for additional licenses. This is a common practice among mortgage brokers. Most focus on the neighboring states when applying for additional licenses. States where the people in your area tend to purchase second homes are also a good choice.

Applying for licenses in neighboring states is a similar process to acquiring a license in your home state. You will need to meet the requirements of the state in which you are seeking the additional license. There is an appendix at the back of this book listing the requirements of each state and contact information to get you started. Keep in mind that some states require a physical office within the state for licensure. In this case, you may not be able to acquire a license in that state and will need to move on to another neighboring state.

Bonds and Minimum Net Worth

A surety bond may be required for the broker to be licensed. A surety bond is a guarantee for the state that the mortgage broker will fulfill his obligations to his clients. It also ensures that the broker will operate according to the rules and regulations of the state. The bond allows clients to recover any losses incurred as a result of the broker from the bond.

If a brokerage firm is operating in more than one state, separate bonds will be needed for each state. The amount of the bond varies from state to state. Typical bond amounts range from $25,000 to $100,000.

A minimum net worth for the broker is sometimes required. Again, the amount of the minimum net worth can vary. A typical range is between $10,000 and $25,000. The net worth of the broker is the difference when all liabilities are subtracted from the broker's assets. The philosophy behind this requirement is that a financially stable broker is more likely to be honest. Whether this holds true or not is up for debate.

Background Investigation

A background investigation is often required for mortgage broker licensing. This will consist of a criminal background check, and applicants will be fingerprinted. The purpose of the background investigation is to ensure the applicant does not have a criminal history. Fraud and other money-related offenses will exclude the candidate from licensing.

Allow plenty of time for the background investigation to be completed when applying for a license. The state will not approve the application without the required background checks. The time it takes varies by state, but it can take a month or more. For example, Colorado requests that applicants allow three months for the background investigation to be completed.

Additional Regulations

Some states have additional regulations that must be met to be licensed as a mortgage broker. A common regulation is that the broker must maintain an office within the state. This means the broker's office or a branch of the company must have a physical location in the state. A post office box is not sufficient, as it must be a physical office where brokers originate loans for clients.

A minimum age requirement will need to be met. This age requirement will be at least 18 years of age. The reason for this requirement is that people under the age of 18 are not allowed to enter into legally binding contracts. Since mortgage brokers enter into a contract with each of their clients, it would be impossible to do business under the legal age of 18 years.

There may be regulations based on citizenship for mortgage brokers. The applicant may be required to be a citizen of the United States. If the person is not a citizen, he or she may be required to have legal status as an alien and be permitted to work in the United States. This prevents unscrupulous people from outside the United States from doing business and causing potential harm to clients.

License Renewal

Continuing Education Units (CEUs) are required for license renewal in many states. This is generally a specific number of hours that must be completed during the licensing period. In some states, this is an annual figure. In other states, the license is good for two or more years and the CEUs must be completed over that two-year period. These states often have more hours needed, since the license is renewed less frequently.

There are solid reasons for requiring CEUs and these benefit the mortgage broker. The courses and workshops taken to fulfill the continuing education requirement keep the mortgage broker up to date on laws in the areas of mortgages and real estate. Laws and regulations change from time to time and CEU classes are a good way to stay abreast of changes that impact the industry.

Common CEU Topics

- Construction loans
- FHA loans
- VA loans
- First-time homebuyers
- Refinancing
- Second mortgages
- Legal issues in the mortgage industry
- Changing regulations on the federal and state level

In most larger and some smaller companies, the firm will track your CEUs for you. Even if your company tracks it for you, it is a good idea to keep your own records as well. Keep copies of all certificates and any other necessary paperwork to prove you attended the training. Keep a log with the dates, times, and topics of the classes and workshops you attend to fulfill the requirements.

The courses you take for your CEUs count as education in your field. Add the courses to the education section of your résumé. This is useful in the event you seek a new job or a client asks to see your résumé. It is also a good place to list the completed mortgage coursework in one place.

FRAGILE

CHAPTER

3

Education & Training

As with licensing, there are benefits to continuing your education as you embark on your career as a mortgage broker. As you increase your knowledge about the mortgage industry, you will be able to provide your clients with better service. This will result in happy clients and more loans closed, which translates into greater income for you. In addition, happy clients are the ones who will talk about you and send business your way. The money spent on education and training pays off with increased business.

Education

There is no specific educational requirement for mortgage brokers. Some have a college degree and others take workshops, online classes, and other certification courses. Workshop-style courses can be found in cities around the country. These vary from basic introductory training to advanced courses for experienced professionals. You can find information on these classes through your local affiliate of the National Association of Mortgage Brokers or on the Internet.

Training and workshops are offered by some employers. These are generally larger companies or mortgage brokerage firms. These classes are convenient and usually can be applied to the CEU requirements of your state. The training covers a wide range of topics, which is great for the new mortgage broker to acquire knowledge of the mortgage industry.

Online training programs can be found around the Internet. The classes and workshops are offered in a variety of formats. Some are conducted in a classroom with several locations. Others are offered on video or DVD. Online workshop materials can be downloaded after the training fee is paid. Some of these courses can be valuable in gaining information about the industry.

You can take these courses for continuing education requirements or for personal knowledge. If planning to use the training to meet the requirements of your state, be sure the course or workshop is approved by your state. When you search for training classes by state, there will be approved courses in the search results.

When selecting a school, certification program, or training course, find out what you are buying because these courses can cost several hundred dollars. Read all the available information and ask questions before you choose a program. Contact information should be included in the advertising or on the Web site for both telephone and e-mail. If the training course will be used to satisfy state requirements for licensing or continuing education, be sure the program or course is approved for the state in which you live.

Certification

Additional certification is available through a variety of sources. Certification is beneficial for the broker. Professional certifications improve the mortgage broker's credibility in the eyes of potential clients and establish a feeling of confidence in the broker. Customers like knowing that their broker has credentials as well as experience.

The National Association of Mortgage Brokers (NAMB) offers three special certification programs. These programs are designed to recognize brokers with varying levels of expertise. These make you stand out among brokers. The programs range from entry-level to programs for experienced professionals.

The exams require anywhere from 0 to 100 qualifying points to be eligible to sit for the exam. The points are awarded by the NAMB depending on a few different factors. A combination of education and work experience is used to determine the points. Entry-level certification requires no points or prior experience.

New brokers start out with the General Mortgage Associate program (GMA). This certification shows potential employers that you have a good knowledge of the mortgage industry and are ready to offer clients quality brokerage services. This credential can set you apart from other people looking for an entry-level job.

To be eligible to take the exam, you must meet a few requirements. The applicant must hold at least a high school diploma or General Equivalency Diploma (GED). Applicants must take and pass the GMA exam within one year of eligibility.

Sign up for the exam on the NAMB Web site (www.namb.net). Choose the testing center that is nearest to your home and the preferred date. The NAMB contracts with a test delivery company to conduct the exam. An e-mail confirmation will be sent after you have registered and paid the fee. The passing score for certification is 68 percent correct answers.

Areas Covered on the GMA Exam

- General knowledge of the mortgage industry
- Mortgage technology
- Business practices and ethics
- Residential financing
- Laws and compliance
- Marketing and sales
- Insurance

There are 125 multiple-choice questions on the exam. A detailed outline of the specific topics covered under each of these seven areas can be found on the NAMB Web site at **http://www.namb.org/images/namb/Certification/GMA/GMA%20Exam%20Content%20Outline.pdf**.

When you feel that you are properly prepared for the test, take a practice run. A practice exam is available on the NAMB Web site for a cost of $29. The practice exam has 55 multiple-choice questions that are derived from the content outline. Take the test online and you will be sent a score report. From this score, you will know which areas need more time in preparation.

The fee for the certification exam is $200 for members or $350 for nonmembers. The cost of NAMB membership depends on the type of membership, but will run a few hundred dollars. There are other benefits in addition to discounts on the exams. A variety of educational courses are offered at state and national events. These cover a wide range of topics and are reasonably priced for members. A subscription to *National Mortgage Broker Magazine* and weekly e-mail newsletters keep the broker up to date on trends and legislative issues.

As mortgage brokers gain experience, there are two other certification levels. The Certified Residential Mortgage Specialist (CRS) certification is for brokers with at least two years of experience and 50 qualifying points. The Certified Mortgage Consultant or (CMC) is the highest level. This exam requires at least five years of experience and 100 qualifying points.

Learn the Local Real Estate Market

The mortgage broker's job is in part tied to the real estate market. Many brokers get a good portion of their business from Realtors and attorneys specializing in real estate. For this reason, it is a good idea to spend some time learning about the local real estate market. While there are classes that you can take, most brokers learn this through independent study.

A good way to get started is to connect with Realtors and home builders in your area. As you get to know these professionals, engage in conversation about the local market, changes, predictions, and any other information you can gather. Realtors and home builders offer a wealth of knowledge about this topic.

Reading publications, trade newspapers, magazines, and newsletters related to the real estate and mortgage market is another way to learn about your local market and stay informed about trends. The *Wall Street Journal* and magazines about economic issues are other good sources of information.

The Internet is another great source of information for mortgage brokers interested in researching the local real estate market. You can study advertisements online as well as in print publications. Watch the real estate listings to see how quickly houses are selling and the value of the homes being sold. You can monitor closings to determine this information.

While you are researching the local real estate market, take some time to inquire about local zoning laws and ordinances that may affect your clients. Home builders are a great source of information on zoning ordinances and recent changes to these ordinances. You can also obtain copies of all zoning ordinances and regulations at your local government office.

CHAPTER 4

Building Business

A large portion of the mortgage broker's time is devoted to finding borrowers to work with. To be successful, the broker needs to close loans. The more loans the broker is able to close, the higher the income potential of that broker. Early in your career, you will spend even more time reaching out to potential clients. Once your business is established, you will still need to recruit new business on an ongoing basis. As current loans are closing, new borrowers are needed to keep the firm moving toward success.

Who Are Your Prospects?

Before you can contact prospective clients, you need a list. Start with your address book and make a list of potential contacts and sources of referrals. Include personal contacts, business contacts, and people that belong to the same clubs and organizations. The lists can be broken down according to category or done in one big list.

Good prospects for leads include:

- Real estate agents
- Financial planners

- Contractors
- Tax accountants
- Lawyers
- Professionals in the banking industry

Once the list is made, look it over carefully to determine who are the best prospects. Review the list and put an asterisk next to the names that are likely to provide a few referrals that can lead to new clients. Ideally, you want to choose people who are likely to provide you with at least a few good leads. This will cut the list down significantly.

Once the list is complete, begin contacting the people on the list. This can be done on the phone or by mail. Explain that you are forming a mortgage broker business and ask if the person is in the market for a mortgage, second mortgage, or refinancing. Ask for referrals from the people on the list. If each person on the list gives just two names, the size of the list will double.

Building a Customer List

Referrals are one of the best ways to build your customer list. To get referrals, you need to request them from people who are likely to have contacts that will benefit the business. Find as many sources as possible to get a greater number of referrals. Professionals in the real estate and mortgage industries can be a good source for leads on potential clients.

Current and past clients are another source of information on potential future clients. When you create or revise your application, add a section for referrals. Ask for a specific number of referrals, rather than a blanket question asking if the client knows anyone in the market for a home loan. Three is a standard number of referrals to ask for on your application.

The mortgage broker can offer incentives for clients to provide referrals. When choosing an incentive for your borrowers, be careful not to violate the Real Estate Settlement Procedure Act (RESPA). RESPA addresses procedures for settlement and closing costs. One portion of RESPA makes kickbacks illegal. This is intended to prevent increases in settlement costs as a result of these kickbacks.

RESPA requires disclosures during the process and a Good Faith Estimate from the broker to the borrower. Cash back to the borrower after closing or a reduction in fees could be a violation of RESPA. Choose incentives that do not violate RESPA or the Good Faith Estimate you provide to your clients. An incentive that is separate from the closing fees or any fees listed on the Good Faith Estimate will keep the broker in compliance with RESPA.

Using Lists From Other Professionals

Initially, the new mortgage broker will not have an extensive list of potential clients. One way to cultivate business while building your own customer list is to borrow lists from other professionals. Choose professionals that are in a related industry, such as real estate, accounting, and home building. These professionals are more likely to provide a list that will result in business for the broker.

Real estate agents are a good source of leads. Realtors deal with people looking to purchase homes on a daily basis. Buyers take the recommendation of their Realtor when they are looking for a mortgage broker to help them secure a loan. To make the most of this source, contact several real estate agencies.

Contractors are another good source of leads for the mortgage broker. Like Realtors, contractors are in touch with people in the market, or soon will be in the market, for a home mortgage. Building homes is their business and they need sources of financing for their customers. Taking the time to develop relationships with a few home builders and contractors in your area will result in a good source of leads.

Tax accountants deal with people and their finances for a living. When talking with their clients, the subject of home mortgages and refinancing comes up often. If you are the go-to guy for that accounting firm, they can send you business on a fairly regular basis. As with Realtors, clients trust the opinion and take the recommendation of the tax accountant when making financial decisions.

Financial planners or financial advisors are professionals that make a living helping clients make sound financial decisions. People turn to these professionals for advice on everything from investments to mortgages. Make contact with a few financial advisors to build your database of potential customers.

Recommendations of family, friends, and professionals are one of the biggest influences for people selecting a broker for a home or commercial mortgage. The opinion of a professional carries the most weight with potential borrowers. Getting business from referrals is more effective than television or print advertising.

Buying Customer Lists

For an even bigger list of prospects, brokers can buy customer lists. Lists are available for anything, including mortgages. There are several ways to go about buying lists. There are companies that exist only to build a database and sell customer lists. Depending on the company and the list, this could be great for the new broker.

Mortgage brokers need to be careful about the lists they purchase. Be sure the list will help you reach your target market, which includes people interested in buying a home, taking a second mortgage, or refinancing their current mortgage. Once you know the clientele you are trying to target, choosing the type of list to buy is easier.

For example, if you want to target people with an adjustable interest rate to get refinancing business, choose a list of people who took an adjustable mortgage a few years ago. Mortgages with a fixed rate for the first few years that change to an adjustable rate get quite expensive. These homeowners will be looking to get out of that expensive loan and this can bring you new borrowers for your business.

There are two different ways to buy leads for your company. One is purchasing a list of potential clients that may be in the market for a home loan. The other is purchasing solid leads that are sold only to you. There is a big difference in terms of the outcome. Buying a list that has been sold to dozens, or even hundreds, of brokers will not bring much new business. In some cases, these potential customers have been contacted so many times that it is unlikely you will get the loan.

When buying lists, you want to be sure the same leads are not being marketed to hundreds of brokers. This is counterproductive and will not lead to more loans closing. Ideally, the best leads are the ones that are only sold to you. The only way to know this is to ask. Before buying any list, speak to someone in the company.

When you speak to the company's representative, ask specific questions to know what you are buying. Ask if the leads are sold over and over again to many brokers. If the representative is not forthcoming or avoids questions, this may not be the best company to work with. Before spending your hard-earned money, be sure the list is worth the money you are spending.

Another option for list buying is to buy lists from professionals in the real estate or finance industries. Some professionals have strict rules about not selling their customer lists, but others have no problem. This is particularly true if the professional thinks the mortgage broker has a valuable service to offer his or her customers.

Buying a list from a professional in one of these industries is likely to be more productive than buying a random list from a company with no experience in real estate or finance. Since the goal is to close more loans, it makes sense to focus on lists that will generate bona fide leads. This method is better in terms of the number of loans that will end up closing. Since brokers get paid according to how many loans they close, buying lists from other professionals is the way to go.

Web Sites Offering Customer Lists for Sale

http://www.wholesalelists.net

This site offers lists specifically designed for mortgage brokers. The company boasts a database of 250 million customers. Lists can be sent on manuscript, mailing labels, CD-ROM, or can be sent to the broker via e-mail.

http://www.eleadspot.com

This site offers live leads to brokers. The company does the cold calling and collects information about the borrower. The call is then transferred to participating brokers to close the deal. This service offers the benefit of prescreening the potential borrowers and only transferring those interested in a mortgage.

http://www.usdatacorp.net/pages/mortgage.php

This is a database of mortgage leads that is useful for finding clients interested in new mortgages, as well as refinancing. Lists are broken down by homeowners, businesses, and specialty markets.

http://www.certified-lists.com/mortgage_lists.htm

This site offers lists based on a wide range of criteria. The broker can get lists of mortgages, second mortgages, loan to value, interest rate, credit history, interest rate, and much more.

How to Use Your List

Once you have built a list of potential clients, it is time to start the contacting process. A good way to make initial contact is by mail or e-mail. Send information about the services you offer and why the potential borrower should use your services over that of another broker. For a better response, send good information that will be of value to the clients you are targeting.

As you build your database of clients and potential clients, stay in touch with the people on your list. Do not assume because leads were not interested in a mortgage when you contacted them that the lead is dead. Circumstances change and the person who had no intention of buying a house or refinancing six months ago may need mortgage services now. Staying in contact keeps your name in the minds of potential clients. When the time comes and they are in the market for a mortgage, it is more likely that they will remember you and give you a call.

There are several ways to stay in contact with potential clients. Send a newsletter that contains information on financing, refinancing, and current interest rates. Any direct mailings or postcards you create can be sent to the people on your contact list. Make sure the information you send is informative and useful to the people on your list.

Newsletters may seem like a time-consuming hassle, but it is worth it in the long run. The mortgage broker that takes the time to cultivate future business will close more loans in the future. You are laying the groundwork for future income. Think of the time and money you spend as an investment in your business.

Talking to Potential Customers

After you have sent information by mail or e-mail, wait for a few weeks to a month. Then begin contacting the people that received your mailings. This is the part of the job that some mortgage brokers cannot stand, but it is necessary. People generally hate sales calls and will initially try to get you off the phone, unless you can get their attention. Do this by offering something they need and showing an interest in the customer.

People like talking about themselves and their families. Rather than spouting off a prewritten sales pitch, take some time to listen to the potential borrower. Get the people talking about their families and their specific needs. As you listen, come up with a program or strategy that meets the needs of the potential borrower. At this point you can begin to turn the conversation to your services and how you can help in their unique situation.

CHAPTER

5

Sales Techniques

It is important to realize that the job of a mortgage broker basically involves sales. The broker is selling his professional services to potential clients who are in the market for a mortgage or want to refinance their homes. Your job is to convince the client you are the right person to help them secure the needed financing. To do this, you will have to sell your service to potential borrowers. How is your business different from every other broker in the phone book? There are several techniques you can use to reach potential clients and make your service stand out from others.

Advertising

A good portion of the mortgage broker's time is spent advertising the service to potential borrowers. Advertising can be done on the Internet, on television, or in print ads. The possibilities for reaching potential clients are endless. There are many things to include in advertisements to convey to borrowers you are an honest and talented mortgage broker. Focus on your service for the best results for your advertising dollar.

Read some advertisements from mortgage brokers. Many include interest rate information in their ads. Some intentionally use a low figure to increase responses to the ad. Then, after a client calls, they inform the customer that the rate stated in the ad is no longer available. The borrower ends up with a rate that is higher than the one in the ad.

In some cases, this scenario is an example of the old "bait and switch" tactic. Lure the customer in with promises of low prices and then inform them that the product they came in for is no longer available. The customer ends up spending more. This tactic has been used in marketing and advertising for many years. To use this tactic is unethical and may be illegal, depending on how it is presented and the intent behind the ad.

Fortunately, most mortgage brokers are honest professionals. However, this does not mean the rate stated in the ad will be available when the borrower arrives. There are many legitimate reasons rates are different than what is stated in the ad. Interest rates fluctuate and may increase from the time the ad was created until it ran in the newspaper. Other differences are generally related to the credit of the borrower and other factors related to the specific mortgage.

For this reason, some mortgage brokers refrain from advertising interest rates. Since rates change and vary by lender and type of loan, it is difficult to use interest rates with a great degree of accuracy. It is better to focus on your expertise and the qualities that make you the best choice for the potential borrower. Build a reputation based on knowledge, skill, and experience rather than relying on interest rates.

Some brokers do use interest rates in their advertising. Sometimes, this is due to the fact that the competitors are using interest rates, and borrowers in the area expect to see this information. In this case, advertise the current rate as accurately as possible. You may want to include a disclaimer about the fluidity of interest rates.

There are laws that regulate how interest rates must be advertised. It is important to follow the guidelines to avoid legal entanglements. Regardless of whether the ad will appear in the newspaper or on your Web site, the requirements are the same. The interest rate cannot be stated without other information. This includes the size of the loan in the scenario depicted in the ad, the term of the loan, and the annual percentage rate. So the ad may say that based on a loan of $300,000 for 30 years, the interest rate is 6 percent. The annual percentage rate must be stated beside the interest rate for full disclosure.

When using interest rates in advertisements, the mortgage broker needs to be prepared to discuss the subject with potential borrowers. Suppose a borrower calls your office with an ad from a competitor showing a lower interest rate. The borrower may want to discuss it with you. In many cases, the loans are completely different. You will need to be able to clearly explain this to potential clients.

Say the ad you are running offers no points or loan origination fees for the borrower. The tradeoff for this is an interest rate that is one half of one percentage point higher. The competitor loan may be charging these fees, but giving a slightly lower rate. When the numbers are crunched, the slightly higher interest rate is often a better deal for borrowers.

The reason it can be a better deal is in the amount of money required up front from the borrower. When there are no points or loan origination fees, less cash is required from the borrower.

Now, the borrower is still paying fees, but in the form of a higher rate of interest over the life of the loan.

When this is explained to the borrower, he will see that the loans are not the same. Some borrowers may not mind putting down several thousand additional dollars to purchase the property, but many would prefer to include the costs in the loan rather than paying them up front. For these customers, the no points or loan origination fee option is the better choice. To effectively explain this difference, the broker needs to be able to do these calculations quickly and accurately.

To get this message across, the mortgage broker needs to speak intelligently about not only the mortgage industry, but financial markets as well. The performance of certain investments and activity in the stock market can affect the interest rate, causing rates to increase or decrease. When the broker is able to explain the underlying economic factors that resulted in the change in rates, the client feels he or she is dealing with a knowledgeable professional.

Testimonials

Using testimonials is one of the most effective marketing strategies a new broker can employ to ensure success. When potential borrowers see testimonials, this adds credibility to the broker's business. If a borrower receives two similar advertisements from mortgage brokers and one has a testimonial and the other does not, the borrower is more likely to choose the services of the company with testimonials from past clients and other professionals.

Because this strategy is so effective, it makes sense to use it in advertising. Include testimonials in print ads, direct marketing, and on your Web site to reap the most benefits from this effective marketing strategy. In a competitive marketplace, this could be the edge a new mortgage broker needs to ensure success.

Another benefit of using testimonials is that they do not cost anything. Advertising to find potential borrowers can be an expensive proposition. Newspaper ads, television and radio spots, direct mailings, and Web sites all cost money. The advertising budget for newer brokers is somewhat limited. Testimonials are free and offer a big payback when used correctly.

To get testimonials, you need to ask for them. Some mortgage brokers feel uncomfortable doing this and do not know where to start. This process is made easier by selecting the right people to ask for testimonials and referrals. The people that should be targeted for testimonials are former clients and professionals in the real estate or finance industry.

These should be people that you have worked with in the past and have had a positive experience with. Start by making a list of prospective people who may give a testimonial and then begin contacting each person on the list. Open the conversation by asking how the person feels about your level of service and their experience in working with you in the past. If the person expresses that they were happy with the level of service, ask for a referral or testimonial.

Using Testimonials

Once you have contacted people and gotten testimonials, it is important to use them in the right way to gain the most advantage.

Always get permission before using the names of former clients or professionals.

Include the credentials of the person writing the testimonial. People are persuaded by credentials. If potential borrowers read a testimonial written by someone in the finance or real estate industry, they are more likely to be impressed by the testimonial than by one written by an anonymous stranger. The person's experience and credentials are important for winning over future borrowers and building a successful business.

Always include a testimonial from a referring professional in all marketing materials. For example, if a tax accountant gives or sells you his list of clients, be sure to use his name and credentials in materials sent to the people on list. Since people tend to trust their financial professionals, seeing his name on the materials you send will go a long way toward building confidence in your service.

Direct Marketing

Direct marketing is marketing directly to the customers you are hoping to attract to your mortgage broker business. Using direct marketing is a skill that can be learned. It is an effective way to reach potential customers and build a successful business. There are businesses that specialize in this type of marketing, but with a little know-how, you can do it and save money.

Examples of Direct Marketing

- Mailed advertisements

- E-mail
- Advertising in a real estate newsletter
- Advertising in newsletters sent by financial professionals
- Postcards
- Coupons sent by mail or e-mail
- Letter introducing yourself and your business to the potential borrower

Direct Mail

Everyone is familiar with direct mail. Chances are you receive direct mail in your mailbox every week. The ads you get from businesses in your local area are examples of direct mail. Although many call this junk mail, it can be advantageous if it is used correctly.

The message is important in direct mail. Be sure the message is tailored to the specific clientele you are hoping to attract. If you specialize in a specific area, such as lower-credit loans, be sure to mention it in the mailer. If you are having trouble crafting a message or just do not know where to start, there are companies that specialize in this business. Consider hiring a professional to help you craft the perfect message to reach your targeted customers.

As you are crafting your message for direct mail, there are a few things to consider. People are more likely to hold on to the mailer and respond when a special offer or other incentive is included in the material. There are a few things you can offer to increase the response to your mailer.

Some brokers offer a free analysis of the customer's financial situation or mortgage market. This is a specific offer to the potential borrower. Yes, it will take the broker some time to put this analysis together, but the cost is minimal for the broker. The customer will be impressed by the personal level of service. Making this connection with the potential borrower can set you apart from other mortgage brokers in your area.

For a more general offer, consider putting together a tutorial that can be sent to potential clients. This could be a series of articles about the current state of the mortgage industry or the variety of loans and programs available to consumers. The series can be requested by the borrower and sent out by the broker through e-mail. Break the series into several components. Send one component each week. This will keep the mortgage broker in the mind of the client.

When using direct mail, it is important to track the responses you get to the ads. Tracking the responses allows the broker to determine which ads are offering a decent return and which are a waste of time, money, and paper. The most successful direct mail campaigns can net a response rate of 40 to 50 percent. Less successful mailers can result in a response rate as low as 10 or even 1 percent.

As you evaluate the response rate of each direct mailing, you will see a pattern. Some are more successful than others. This information can be used to help develop future direct mailers. The mortgage broker will be able to concentrate on the type of mailings that bring a good result and avoid repeating ones that result in little or no response.

If the mortgage broker includes an incentive in direct mail, tracking the response is easier. Use a different incentive in each mailing to make tracking it easier. For example, on one mailer, offer a free analysis of the current mortgage market and on another use a free analysis of the borrower's financial situation. On a third, offer a tutorial on the loans and programs available to borrowers. When the offers are redeemed, you can count which were the most successful. This makes planning future direct mail campaigns easier.

E-mail Marketing

E-mail marketing is direct marketing without the mail. Direct marketing messages are sent to the inbox of targeted borrowers in a similar way to traditional mailing of advertisements to potential clients. This method of reaching potential clients is becoming increasingly popular for several reasons. Sending messages via e-mail allows the mortgage broker to reach a larger number of potential borrowers at a lower price than traditional mailers.

A newsletter sent via e-mail is an example of e-mail marketing. Do not send newsletters more than twice a month to avoid irritating potential clients. In addition, include information that is interesting to read and offers valuable information to potential borrowers. Include articles that are relevant to the mortgage industry, tips for finding a loan, credit repair information, or any other relevant topic. Be sure the articles are well written, sound professional, and do not contain any spelling or grammar mistakes.

When crafting e-mail marketing messages, be sure to include links to the Web site. Your subscribers can click the link for more information about you and your business. Include links to the home page and other relevant pages throughout the message. In many cases, targeted customers do not click the first link, but will click on a link later in the message.

The success of e-mail marketing messages can be tracked by click-through statistics. The number of people that click on the link and number of e-mail messages sent are used to calculate the click-through rate. If you are using more than one message in your e-mail marketing campaign, you can compare the click-through rates to determine which messages are most effective. This is useful in crafting future messages since you know which resulted in the greatest number of responses.

When planning and implementing e-mail marketing, be sure not to violate antispam laws. The United States has the Controlling the Assault of Non-Solicited Pornography and Marketing Act, also known as the CAN-SPAM Act. This 2003 law sets standards for sending commercial e-mail.

However, there are provisions that allow businesses to send unsolicited e-mail, if certain conditions are met. The message must have a subject line that is not misleading or deceptive about the contents of the message and be identified as an advertisement. Also, it must include a valid postal address and the recipients of the message must have an option to opt out of future advertisements. When a consumer chooses to opt out, the business has ten days to comply with that request.

The CAN-SPAM Act does not apply to e-mail messages sent to a business's customers or visitors that opt in to e-mail messages on a Web site. For example, if you offer an e-mail newsletter, visitors to your site can subscribe. These e-mail addresses can then be used for any e-mail marketing without fear of violating the law.

The law is enforced by the Federal Trade Commission (FTC). The penalty for violating the act is a fine of up to $11,000 per violation. The severity of the penalty depends on the specific offense. Sending a message with a false or misleading subject line is a misdemeanor. Other practices such as harvesting, hijacking computers, and IP address spoofing are considered aggravated offenses.

Web Sites

In the past, a Web site was a nice extra for the mortgage broker. Now it is a necessity. People are so used to being able to visit a Web site for more information that now they are suspicious or turned off if there is not one available. The time and money invested in setting up a professional-looking Web site are well worth it in the long run.

There is no reason not to have one. Web sites are fairly inexpensive and easy to set up. If you are computer savvy, you may be able to do it on your own. Otherwise, make an investment in a company that specializes in Web site development. The startup cost is a couple thousand dollars, but this is a one-time expense.

The monthly maintenance fees are not unreasonable and help make the broker look professional. Look for a company that includes a few updates with the monthly or annual fee. You will want to keep the site updated and fresh, rather than having it look dated or neglected.

Things to include on the Web site:

- Information on the mortgage broker, education, licensing, and experience
- Articles about the mortgage industry and refinancing
- E-mail link to contact you
- Guest book
- Forward feature to send the Web site to a friend
- Mortgage calculator
- Information on current interest rates

The Web site address should be included on all direct marketing, your business card, and any other literature you hand out to potential clients. A Web site is great for customers to learn more after reading a direct mailer or sales letter. If you want your Web site to attract borrowers as well as offer potential borrowers more information on your business, you will need to spend some time and money marketing your Web site.

People have become accustomed to searching online for information. This includes looking for a mortgage broker. A Google search for mortgage brokers gives over 8 million results. With this number of Web sites, yours can get lost. If you are on page 64, few borrowers will ever see your site, unless they have the exact address. The only way for people to see your Web site is to improve the ranking in the search engines.

Improving Search Engine Ranking

To be seen by potential borrowers, your Web site needs to be listed on the first few pages. For best results, it is important to get the Web site on the first page. To increase your ranking, the right keywords need to be used. Search engines use keywords to identify and categorize the Web site in the listing. Choosing the right keywords is critical to getting a higher ranking in the search engines.

When selecting keywords, stay away from generic words and phrases like "mortgage broker." So many Web sites are already using this phrase that your site will be lost in the shuffle. Choose more specific keywords and phrases to achieve a higher ranking. Software tools are available to help in selecting keywords.

The content on the Web site can be optimized using many different keyword combinations. Build the Web site with rich content and use the keyword combinations to increase search engine ranking. The best way to do this is to use more pages that are rich in content, which can be done with articles. Write articles or hire a freelance writer who is experienced in search engine optimization. The writer can build the articles around specific keyword combinations.

The more content that you have on your Web site, the greater the opportunity you have to use keyword optimization. Craft your content carefully to make the most of this strategy. Quality content has another benefit. Visitors to the Web site will stop to read the articles to obtain information about mortgages and refinancing. When the information in the articles is high quality, this speaks highly of the mortgage broker. This can translate into more loans closing and greater success.

Inbound links are another way to increase a Web site's ranking in the search engine and to drive more traffic to the site. Linking from other Web sites is like networking on the Internet. Links on other Web sites bring traffic to your site. Software is available that finds and creates quality links to your Web site.

This software is fairly ingenious. It locates links to competitor sites and finds quality Web sites to link to yours. Software for link promotion and management is not expensive. A good program costs a few hundred dollars, which is a small investment to bring traffic to the Web site.

The best way to get at the top of the rankings is to pay for that service. The top of the page is always held by paid subscribers. The more you pay, the higher ranked the site. There are a few ways to do this. One is to pay for relevant search advertising. The link to your Web site is located on pages with relevant search content. This is among the most expensive ways to get a high ranking, but it is effective.

Another way to do it is known as pay-per-click. There is a set amount of money charged each time someone clicks the link to the Web site. The more clicks, the higher the monthly fee. Google AdWords is an example of pay-per-click. This can get expensive if many users click on your site.

There is a local search option when using pay-per-click advertising. For example, if a potential borrower in your area is searching for mortgage brokers, they will see the link to your Web site. This is an effective way to reach borrowers in your area. The amount of money charged for each click is lower with the local search option, which can save you money and result in more borrowers in your area finding the Web site.

Marketing Yourself

As a mortgage broker, you are selling a service: helping people find a mortgage. However, it is not only your service that you are selling as you are selling yourself to potential borrowers. Why should a potential borrower choose you over the other mortgage brokers in your area? What is unique about you or the service you offer?

In marketing, this is referred to as your unique selling proposition, or USP. Basically the USP is a short statement or slogan used in advertising to set your mortgage broker service apart from the competition. The first step is to figure out a USP that fits. Do not shoot for the moon and make a far-out claim, such as claiming you can get a loan for any borrower. Instead, make it a statement you can fulfill.

There are a few ways to arrive at a USP. One that is becoming more popular involves demographics. You may have seen businesses advertised as locally owned. People like working with businesses that are part of the local community. They also see stability in a locally owned business and want to patronize them.

Determine the needs of the customers you are hoping to attract. What do they need? How can you fill that need? Statements such as "expert in refinancing" or "tough credit loans" set you apart as experienced in certain areas. This will resonate with people looking for a loan that fits that criterion.

When crafting your USP, write a short statement. Ideally, the USP should be shorter than a sentence. This makes it more likely to be remembered by potential borrowers. The USP should also be specific. Think of advertising slogans that become synonymous with a product or company, such as Domino's 30-minute delivery guarantee or FedEx for when it has to be there overnight.

These businesses have built a solid reputation on their USP. Craft a unique statement about your service that will keep you in the minds of potential borrowers. Once you have determined your USP, it is important to put it to use. Be sure to include the USP in all advertising, by mail, online, and in print.

Developing a Marketing Strategy

Your USP, advertising, Web site, and print and e-mail marketing are all part of your overall marketing strategy. Rather than sending out random advertisements, spend time putting together an overall strategy. This helps the mortgage broker target the intended audience and gives a blueprint for future advertising.

Who do you want to reach? Sit down with paper and a pen and determine your target market. Once you have determined who you are trying to reach, you can begin to develop a marketing strategy that will help you successfully reach your target market. How can you best use your resources to reach these people? This will help you determine where to spend your advertising dollars.

Where can your potential borrowers be found? Are they more likely to respond to print, radio ads, television spots, or online marketing? For example, a mortgage broker looking to target first-time home buyers may want to put more effort into building a Web site and other methods of online marketing. Since younger people tend to spend a lot of time on the Internet, they will find their way to your Web site and you.

However, if you are planning to advertise to the older market, advertising on the Web may not be as profitable. For example, if you are advertising home equity loans or refinancing to older workers or retired people, realize that this group does not spend as much time finding information on the Internet. They will respond better to traditional direct mail or advertisements on radio and television.

Pay attention to advertising by the competition. Visit sites of other brokers and read advertisements in the newspaper and magazines. What are they doing? What is good about it and what is not good? Consider what they are doing well and how you can improve upon it. This is a good jumping-off point, especially for newer mortgage brokers.

Before you start purchasing ad space and air time, consider how much you can afford to spend. Set a budget for advertising, as this budget will help you keep track of expenses and not spend more than you can comfortably afford. Later, as your business grows and you become successful, you can expand the budget for future advertising campaigns. Keep in mind that advertising is an ongoing proposition and changes can be made as needed.

Tracking the Success of Your Plan

Track the success of your marketing plan. On your application, include a space asking how the borrower learned about your business. This can be a few blank lines for the borrower to fill in or a box with choices, such as Web site, radio, newspaper ad, and any other advertising method you use to promote your business. The borrower checks the appropriate box on the application.

This allows you to determine which advertising methods were most effective. This is helpful for setting a future advertising budget. You can figure out which advertising methods offer the biggest return on your investment. This helps you determine where future monies are best spent. If one particular method of advertising did not bring any borrowers to your door, you may want to drop it and choose another method in its place.

If you want more detailed information, you can analyze it a bit further. A good way to determine the effectiveness of any marketing strategy is to calculate the cost per lead. How many leads is a source generating each month? How much did you spend for an advertising campaign or marketing strategy and how many good leads did you get from it? This will help you determine how much money each lead cost.

You can break this down even further, although doing so does require a bit more work. However, if the result is a more streamlined and successful marketing strategy, the money spent will be well worth it. Some of the things you can track is how many of these leads resulted in a loan that went to closing. Also, what was the cost per closing? This is a better indication of actual income to you than the cost-per-lead method.

Evaluate your sources of referrals periodically as well. How many are you getting? Where are these leads originating? Make a list of the sources of referrals and how many potential loans and closings resulted from each. This will help you see where you have experienced success, which will help you plan for the future. If you find that a certain group of professionals is sending the most leads, you may want to cultivate more relationships with other professionals in the same industry.

Concentrate your future budget on the most successful advertising methods based on previous marketing campaigns. Trying to do it all and running ads in every potential media outlet results in spreading the budget too thin. Marketing research shows that customers often need to hear about a product or service many times before making a purchase or using a service.

For this reason, it is important to get your message out there and keep it that way. This is easier to accomplish when you are concentrating on a few advertising methods. Rather than hearing the message once, potential borrowers have the opportunity to hear it several times. Most people do not respond the first time they are confronted with an advertisement, whether on the radio, on television, or in a print ad. The same customer, after hearing your message several times, is more likely to call your office or visit your Web site.

Marketing is a long-term investment. As loans close, the mortgage broker needs new borrowers. You want to continually evaluate the effectiveness of each component of your overall marketing plan. When a specific type of advertisement brings results, use this method in the future. When an advertisement falls flat and brings no business, make a change.

HOUSE
FOR SALE
BY OWNER

CHAPTER

6

Income

The mortgage lending industry is huge. In 2004, there were over $1.8 trillion dollars in loan transactions. Using a 1 percent commission for mortgage brokers, the figure for total commissions paid in 2004 is over $18 billion dollars. The income potential for new mortgage brokers is nearly limitless. The more loans you close and the greater the value of the loans for those homes, the more income you will earn. Therefore, the goal is to build your business so you have a steady stream of loans closing.

Average Income of Mortgage Brokers

According to the November 2005 issue of *Broker* magazine, the average salary for a mortgage broker was $103,507. This average includes the high-earning brokers and those brand new in the industry. For the starting broker, annual salaries between $40,000 and $50,000 are not unusual.

It is not always easy to determine the average salary of mortgage brokers. This statistic varies according to several factors. One of the factors that has a big influence on the amount of money a broker earns is the area in which the broker works. A mortgage broker working in an area that is in demand and has decent property values will earn more than a broker working in a less desirable area with lower priced homes.

Since mortgage brokers are paid on commission, the number of loans closed will have the biggest impact on the income of the broker. Closing two or three loans in a month will result in a salary of only around $30,000. For most mortgage brokers, this is not considered enough. To increase the annual salary, the broker needs to close more loans.

Income varies according to the type of loan. Certain loans, such as nonconforming, no-doc, undocumented income, and low credit score earn more money for the mortgage broker. These loans are more difficult to secure and require more work on the part of the broker. For this reason, brokers charge more in terms of fees. As a result of the higher fees, the broker makes more money.

Fees Charged by Mortgage Brokers

The main fee that constitutes the income of the mortgage broker is the brokerage fee. This fee is a percentage of the amount of the loan. It is often expressed as points. One point is 1 percent of the loan amount. The range in this fee is usually between 1 and 2 percent. The percentage is higher based on the difficulty of securing the loan.

There are two ways this can work for the borrower. The borrower may want a lower interest rate and will pay more in fees to the broker and the lender. This method requires more money down on the mortgage from the borrower. Some borrowers prefer to have a slightly higher interest rate and pay less at the closing table. In this case, part or all of the broker's fees will be paid by the lender. The lender then recoups that money by collecting more on monthly payments due to the higher interest rate.

Another somewhat controversial fee is the yield spread premium (YSP). This has been getting attention due to the problems in the subprime market. The YSP works similar to taking a higher interest rate in exchange for fewer upfront costs. This is often done on the subprime market where the borrower cannot afford the upfront fees from the broker or lender.

The broker offers the borrower a slightly higher interest rate. The broker is then paid by the lender in the form of an YSP, rather than by the borrower at closing. The fees are spread out over the life of the mortgage, saving the borrower money at closing.

The controversy over YSP money paid by the lender to the broker surrounds the disclosure to the borrower. In some cases, class action suits have been filed because the process was not disclosed to borrowers and excessive fees were charged. By law, brokers must disclose their fees to borrowers. In addition, a few unscrupulous lenders and brokers charged exorbitant fees, leaving borrowers with higher interest rates than necessary.

This practice hurts the borrower and damages the credibility of mortgage brokers. To uphold the respect of the brokerage industry and your own personal reputation, you will want to disclose all information. This is done with a Good Faith Estimate, a document required by law.

Good Faith Estimates

The mortgage broker can avoid accusations of charging excessive fees and protect his professional reputation by following all regulations regarding the Good Faith Estimate. A mortgage broker is required to provide the borrower with a Good Faith Estimate within three days from the time the borrower signs the application.

Fees on a Good Faith Estimate

- Loan origination fee
- Loan discount
- Appraisal fee
- Credit report
- Lender's inspection fee
- Mortgage broker fee
- Tax-related service fee
- Processing and underwriting fees
- Fees for closing and title company
- Taxes and insurance premiums that will be held in escrow by the lender
- Document preparation fees
- Recording fees
- Inspection fees

This is an estimate and actual fees may differ. When the borrower works with a mortgage broker, they will actually get two estimates: one from the broker and one from the lender. The Good Faith Estimate from the broker can state that a lender has not been determined. The later Good Faith Estimate from the lender will contain the lender's fees.

Some of the fees will remain the same, regardless of the lender. These include fees related to document preparation, notary fees, insurance, and taxes. The Good Faith Estimate should contain a reasonable estimate of these costs, whether or not a lender has been contacted regarding the borrower.

The money you earn on the loan will be shown under mortgage broker fees. Since the loan has not been secured yet, the fee is an approximation based on the estimated size of the loan. In the interest of full disclosure, include both the dollar amount and percent of the home loan, for example 1 percent.

Why It Is a Good Idea to Guarantee Your Fees

Customers feel more comfortable with a guarantee. By guaranteeing your fees, you build your reputation and generate more business and client referrals. There are many benefits to this word of mouth. People talk about their experiences when buying a home. They talk about experiences, good and bad. They are more likely to talk about bad experiences to a greater number of people.

When a borrower works with an honest mortgage broker, they are likely to recount this experience to friends, family members, and coworkers. If the experience is good, this can generate future business for the mortgage broker. Offering a detailed list of fees up front and standing by those fees is a good way to promote goodwill and increase business.

How to Guarantee the Fees

Guaranteeing your fees does not cost you a thing and makes a difference in how you are perceived by potential borrowers. Since your Good Faith Estimate is based on the amount of the loan, the fee should be accurate. State the fee as both a dollar amount and a percentage of the loan. Once this amount has been determined, it is not likely to change.

The only time the fees would change is if, for example, the borrower changes his mind right after signing the Good Faith Estimate and selects a different house for purchase. If the house is more expensive, your fees would be higher. In this case, a new Good Faith Estimate would be prepared. Other costs, such as property tax, insurance, and other fees will change as well. This would all be reflected on the new estimate.

Some brokers also guarantee the lender's fees. The customer is guaranteed that the lender's fees will not increase higher than the number the mortgage broker told the borrower. If the lender's fees are higher than what is stated, the broker guarantees the difference. This is a "peace of mind" guarantee that does not cost much. Once the lender has been identified and states the fees to the broker, there is rarely a problem.

When guaranteeing fees to potential borrowers, be sure to make it clear that the interest rate is not guaranteed. Interest rates change frequently, as the rate of the loan can fluctuate with the market until the customer locks in the rate. As a result of the changing interest rates, no guarantee should be made with regard to interest rates.

Sources of Income

Most, if not all, of the mortgage broker's income is paid based on a percentage of the total fees collected. This money is split between the mortgage broker and the brokerage firm. This percentage is often between 40 and 80 percent. There are several factors that influence the percentage paid to the broker.

The experience of the broker is one of the biggest factors companies use to determine the split. A new broker will get a smaller percentage than the more experienced brokers employed by the same company. One reason for this is the cost to the employer of training and mentoring the broker. The more supervision that is required, the more of the company's resources are spent. This money is recouped by offering a smaller percentage on the new broker's loan closings. As the broker gains experience, his percentage increases.

The type of loan influences the percentage of the commission the broker earns on a loan. Conforming loans, such as conventional mortgages, require less work on the part of the broker. The same is true for refinance loans and second mortgages, provided the borrower has a good credit rating. Nonconforming loans, such as jumbo loans and loans with poor credit, take more time and effort on the part of the broker. It is common for fees to be higher with these types of loans.

Some loan programs available to borrowers affect the percentage paid to the broker. Federal Housing Authority (FHA) and Veterans Administration (VA) loans have requirements that are different from other loan programs. Courses are available to learn to navigate the processes of the FHA and VA. Taking these classes and becoming knowledgeable in this area could result in a slightly higher percentage paid to the mortgage broker from the brokerage company.

Many companies use the size of the loan as a factor in determining the percentage. There are a wide variety of percentage structures used by different brokerage firms. In general, loans over one million dollars are paid a higher commission. Since the commission charged by the company is higher, the broker is eligible for more compensation. This structure can be lucrative if working in an area with high home values.

In addition to the percentage split, there are other sources of income for the mortgage broker. Companies offer bonuses or incentive programs to help increase profit. The company may do this if they are pushing certain loan types or programs. For example, a company may decide they want to increase the number of jumbo loans or refinance loans. They may decide to offer an incentive by making this a part of the goals set for mortgage brokers within the firm.

The bonus will usually be tied to certain performance goals. Factors such as the total loan volume and number of loans closed are common goals set for broker performance. The amount paid in the bonus will be dependent upon the broker meeting or exceeding the goals set by the company. The bonus structure varies from company to company. Bonuses can be paid monthly, quarterly, semi-annually, or annually.

Additional bonuses and incentives are offered to the sales managers in most brokerage firms. These programs are usually based on a commission for every loan closed by the mortgage brokers the manager supervises. The more loans the brokers close, the larger the incentive paid to the sales manager.

Income Potential

Since mortgage brokers earn a living based on the number of loans closed, there is no limit on the amount of income that can be earned. Increase the volume of loans and the broker's salary will increase. One way to do this is to increase the number of loan closings per month. The more loans that close, the more money the broker will earn in commission.

A broker closing two or three loans each month can expect to earn about $30,000. If that broker closes 15 loans each month, he can expect to earn about $150,000. There will be slow periods and busy times, but aiming for at least 15 loans per month is a good goal for attaining success as a mortgage broker.

Another way to increase income is to increase the size of the loans. Since the broker's commission is based on the size of the loans, larger loans result in larger commissions. There is a higher income potential in high-priced real estate markets. The broker can earn the same amount or more in commissions without increasing the number of loans closed in a month.

Tips for Maximizing Income

Specialize in a particular area to increase your income as a mortgage broker. If you can get into the position of being the go-to guy for a specific type of loan, referrals from real estate agents, contractors, and accountants will increase dramatically. There are several areas in which a broker can specialize, such as low credit loans, nonconforming loans, and no-doc loans.

The key to choosing a specialty is to think about the borrower you want to target. What are the needs of that borrower? Make a list of the needs of borrowers in a few niche markets. How can you best meet the needs of these borrowers? Figure out the need and then offer a service to meet that need.

Specializing in mortgages for self-employed individuals is great for increasing referrals from other professionals. Self-employed borrowers often run into trouble qualifying for certain programs. These borrowers often benefit from no-doc or no-income-verification loans. Make connections with lenders that are receptive to self-employed borrowers to help establish yourself as a specialist in this area.

Consider working in the commercial market, rather than strictly with residential loans. The mortgage market for residential loans is dependent upon the economy. Changes in economic factors, the real estate market, and interest rates all have an impact on the number of home sales. This affects the income of mortgage brokers. The same is not true for the commercial market.

Moving from the residential into the commercial market is not easy. The right training and knowledge of the commercial mortgage market is critical to success. There are classes in commercial mortgage brokering. These are valuable for gaining the knowledge you need for success.

There are several things a commercial mortgage broker needs

to know. One important factor is knowledge of the commercial lending industry. There are a large number of different types of loans for commercial real estate. These loans are not all available from one lender, as is common in residential mortgages. Each lender works with different types of loans and has unique programs. The broker needs to make contacts with these lenders to offer the best service to borrowers.

The mortgage process is different with commercial loans. The required documents are different and more detailed. A business plan, letters, executive summaries, and other documents may be required, depending on the lender. The summaries are important and must be written correctly because poorly written executive summaries can cause the loan to be lost. The process is not only more involved, but takes longer as well.

Consider working with an experienced commercial broker, as you would with a residential broker. In some states, a separate broker's license is needed for commercial loans. Determine what is required in your state by contacting the licensing bureau. Information on licensing for each state is located in the back of this book in the appendix.

In many states, the broker can work under the company's license while applying for the necessary licensing. While you are preparing to take the test, you can get started under the supervision of an experienced broker. Once you have received the necessary training and licensing, you can work on your own. In the meantime, working with an experienced broker is a great way to learn the commercial mortgage industry.

CHAPTER 7

How to Locate Borrowers

Locating borrowers is a continual concern for mortgage brokers. Throughout your entire career as a mortgage broker, a considerable portion of your time will be spent in locating future clients. As loans close, you need new clients to begin working on the next loan. Over time, you will build a reputation in the community and network with a larger number of clients and professionals.

Cultivating relationships with other professionals is a good way to get continual referrals. Concentrate on professionals in the real estate and financial industries to get quality leads. These are leads that are likely to result in a closing. Joining your local chamber of commerce and other business organizations is a good way to connect with people in a variety of industries. Attend meetings regularly and get to know the professionals in your area to begin building your reputation as a qualified professional.

Realtors

Realtors are the most obvious professionals for mortgage brokers to work with, as they have access to borrowers on a daily basis.

People who are shopping for a house are usually in the market for a mortgage as well. Get to know the Realtors in a few different offices in your area to get great leads. Working with several different offices will help increase the number of high-quality leads for your business.

Begin by making sales calls to the real estate office. This is known as cold calling and many new brokers hate doing it. In fact, most sales professionals hate cold calling, regardless of the industry or product they are selling. In your case, as a mortgage broker, you are selling yourself to Realtors. The first step in this process is to get to know them.

Stop by on a regular basis to touch base with them. In some cases, you may be able to attend a sales meeting or other event. Offer to give a short talk on the current trends in the mortgage market or predictions for interest rates and home sales. This information is valuable to the Realtor and, by giving the meeting, you increase your credibility with the agents in the office. The next time they are talking to a borrower about mortgage brokers, your name will come to mind.

Ask if you can leave literature in the office for Realtors to share with home buyers. Leave some brochures and business cards. When Realtors makes a recommendation, they will have literature to give the borrower. Include your Web site and e-mail address on all brochures and business cards for the borrower to make contact. Other items, such as refrigerator magnets, pens, or magnetic calendars, are inexpensive handouts to include with your other literature. These can be ordered online through many vendors at reasonable prices.

In some cases, Realtors will let a mortgage broker participate in an open house in the area. The broker sets up a small table with information about mortgages in a corner of the house. As people come through to look at the house, they may stop and talk to you about financing their purchase. Bring along brochures, business cards, and any other literature you may have. Consider investing in give away items, such as pens with your name and phone number to use at these events.

Financial Planners

Financial planners or financial consultants can be a great source of leads. Financial planners help their clients with all aspects of their financial life. It is typical for clients to ask for advice about a wide variety of investments, including mortgages. When this happens, the ideal situation for you is to be the first person that comes to the financial planner's mind. It is beneficial to cultivate relationships with financial planners or advisors in your area.

The referrals from financial planners are generally quality referrals. The clients they refer are ready to buy a house and are likely to use the broker referred by their financial advisor. People place a great deal of trust in the person handling their financial investments. Leads from financial planners are likely to result in closings without a great deal of effort on your part.

Make connections with financial planners at chamber of commerce meetings. You can also solicit the professionals, set an appointment with them, and discuss your experience and what you have to offer their clients. You want to be able to discuss current trends in mortgages as well as other elements of the financial market.

Financial professionals will be impressed by a broker with a clear understanding of the market and will easily spot one who does not have this knowledge.

The nice thing about connecting with financial planners is that there is less competition from other brokers. Realtors, contractors, and even accountants get solicited by brokers to varying degrees, which means more people are going after the same leads as you. Far fewer people are connecting with professionals in the finance industry. Taking advantage of this relatively untapped market can generate high-quality leads on a regular basis.

Tax Accountants

Tax accountants are another group of professionals that a mortgage broker wants to know. Like financial planners, accountants are privy to a lot of financial information. They often discuss mortgages with clients and the tax advantages of home ownership. It is natural for clients to ask their tax accountants for information about home mortgages. The referrals the broker gets from accountants tend to be high-quality leads.

You can meet accountants as you would other professionals in your area. Many CPAs and owners of small accounting firms belong to the chamber of commerce. You may get the opportunity to network with a few accountants by attending regular meetings. As you get to know each other over a period of months, you are likely to get quality referrals on a regular basis.

When talking to accountants, you want to be prepared. Ideally, you should be comfortable talking about the financial aspects of mortgages and the current state of affairs in the mortgage industry.

Be ready to do some quick calculations because accountants are numbers people. If you want to impress them, show that you know your stuff. The accountant will be more comfortable referring a client to you.

You should also be prepared to discuss tax laws that affect real estate and mortgages. The subject of discussion between tax accountants and clients is in the area of tax law and tax benefits. You want to show your knowledge and expertise in these areas to gain referrals from tax professionals.

When reaching out to tax accountants, start with your own. It is likely that you already know him and will feel comfortable with the conversation. If you can get him to send you a few referrals and you do a great job, more leads will come. In addition, your accountant may then recommend your service to other tax accountants for their clients. This can cause the number of leads from accountants each month to grow substantially.

Other Professionals

Contractors and home builders are good sources for referrals. They work every day with people who intend to build a new home. As a result, they have a steady stream of potential borrowers that could be sent your way. It will take some time and effort to gain the confidence of builders, but it is well worth it in the end. Next to Realtors, this group of professionals may be your best bet for a high volume of leads.

The competition for home builders and contractors may be steep. Many already have a mortgage broker they use, or more than one. In this case, work may be available when the primary broker has enough open loans and the contractor has one that cannot wait. Then, as you do a few loans, the builder will get to know you and your level of service. If your service is excellent, you may find more referrals coming your way.

Attorneys are another source of referrals. People talk with their attorneys about a wide range of things. If the attorney handles financial matters for the borrower, he may ask the attorney for information about where to find a mortgage or home loan. Taking the time to make a connection with a few attorneys can bring referrals.

Finding a Niche Market

In business terms, a niche market is a specific segment of a target market that has needs that are not being addressed by the general market. For a mortgage broker, this means a group of borrowers who have a specific need in terms of home financing and that need is not being met by other brokers. Having a niche market is a great way to generate leads and increase loan closings.

An example of a niche market is the United States military. Military personnel may need home loans. They do not always live on base and even if they do, they will look to purchase a home after their tour of duty is complete. Reach out to members of the military in advertisements and on your Web site. Offer information about VA loan programs as well as other relevant mortgage information. Similar niche markets can be found in community service jobs, such as loans for teachers, police officers, or other professions.

Start by brainstorming for niche marketing opportunities in your area. What are some of the groups that you could target as a niche market? Make a list of these groups. Ideally, the groups you list should be large enough to bring in a significant and continual stream of loans, resulting in more opportunity and income for you. The group should also have adequate income to be able to qualify for home loans; otherwise you are wasting your time.

Look at your list of potential groups for niche marketing. Consider which offer the best opportunity for growing your business. Next, consider which groups you would best fit in with. Where are you most comfortable? Since a large portion of your job is in communicating with new and potential clients, you want to feel comfortable interacting with the people in your niche group.

Self-employed people are a concern to financial professionals. Often tax accountants and financial planners deal with self-employed individuals. These people tend to have difficulty in finding a mortgage. If you can establish yourself in the market of brokering for self-employed people, this will make you stand out to tax accountants and other financial professionals.

Mortgage companies are set up for people that work for an employer. The documentation and work history requested by lenders is geared toward individuals with traditional jobs. If an individual is self-employed, income becomes a bit more difficult to verify. When the income is sufficient, it is not always seen as dependable by the lender. This is a big hurdle for self-employed borrowers.

This is a hurdle, but not an insurmountable one. A good mortgage broker can mean the difference between having a loan approved or denied. As the mortgage broker, you can help put together a great package to present to the lender that will allay fears of the borrower having an undependable source of income.

One of the first steps in the income verification process for self-employed people is to get a letter or statement from the tax accountant. This letter helps to verify that the borrower has had a steady source of income over the past few years. Typically, lenders look at the previous two years. Some savvy future homeowners know this already and seek the letter and advice from their tax accountants. This is where the work you have done to connect with the accountant will pay off. He will send the client to you for help in securing a home loan.

The problem of income verification is an issue, even when the self-employed borrower makes more money than an employee collecting a salary who does similar work. When faced with two borrowers, one with a steady job and the other self-employed, lenders have traditionally preferred the borrower with a steady paycheck. This is true even when the paycheck is far smaller.

To succeed in this or any niche market, you need to know your market inside and out. Spend some time reading publications for self-employed business owners and learn the tax laws that are relevant to this target market. When you speak to potential borrowers, you want to sound like an expert. You are selling your expertise, so be sure to cultivate your knowledge on this subject.

With 12.2 million self-employed business owners in the United States, this is a huge market for the mortgage broker. There are millions of potential borrowers who have obstacles, but a talented broker can help them overcome these. If you can establish yourself in this market, the number of leads you will get from tax and financial professionals will increase dramatically.

Some lenders are beginning to realize the significance of this untapped market. Some companies are beginning to offer loan programs directed to the self-employed. Lenders are institutions with money that they want to lend. As the mortgage broker, it is your job to contact lenders and find these programs for your self-employed clients. This is where making connections with several lenders pays off.

Some lenders are responding to this need by offering mortgage loan programs specifically for self-employed individuals. These programs have less stringent requirements for income verification. Some programs require fewer supporting documents and will accept letters from current clients to show stability in the borrower's business. Other programs allow the borrower to certify to the lender that the income reported to the lender is true and accurate.

Some lenders offer loan programs to self-employed individuals that allow for fluctuations in monthly income. Certain fields, such as tax accountants and contractors, have busy seasons and slow seasons. The money earned in the busy months carries the business owner through the leaner months of the year. In these loan programs, flexible payment options are included. These allow the borrower to make larger payments in the busy months and smaller ones in the months when work is typically slow. By the end of the year, the total amount paid is the same, just in different monthly installments that benefit these professionals.

Even lenders without these programs can be swayed with a solid application package that contains several elements. Basically, you need to show the lender that the borrower has a steady stream of income. This can be done by showing certain financial records. One of these is audited financial statements from the past several years. Traditionally, lenders want to see the work history for the past two years. When the borrower is self-employed, include financial information for the past three years.

These audited financial statements would be prepared by the borrower's tax accountant. The problem with these statements is that the main purpose of the tax accountant is to save the taxpayer as much money as possible in taxes. To do this, the accountant has worked hard to offset expenses in an effort to reduce tax liability. The result of this action is that the borrower's net profit – and as a result, income – is significantly less.

Loan programs available for self-employed borrowers, whether through special programs or traditional loans, vary according to several factors. The income level of the borrower, the loan-to-value ratio of the property, and the credit score of the borrower are a few of these factors. Learn as much as possible about the loan programs available to best serve your clients and to establish yourself as an expert in this large and lucrative niche market.

CHAPTER 8

Referrals

Mortgage brokers, like all business owners, spend a significant amount of money attracting new business. The irony is that the best source of advertising will not cost you a dime out of your advertising budget. Referrals are more effective than any other type of advertising. A referral is the best possible way to get a serious client. To achieve success as a mortgage broker, you need to network to generate a steady stream of referrals.

There are several benefits to the broker when working with clients who have been referred, rather than clients that respond to advertising. A potential borrower who sees your ad and calls your office does not know anything about you. He is most likely shopping for the lowest rate and is calling other brokers and banks.

You will need to work to sell your unique service to these clients, compared to those who have been referred to your office. The client that has been referred is more likely to view you as a professional and to trust your judgment. A friend or family member has already sold this person on your service. Your job is half done by the time the person picks up the phone to call you.

How and Where to Get Referrals

There are two good ways to generate referrals: from past clients and professionals. The best way to get referrals from clients is by request. A good time to do this is when the loan closes. The borrower is likely happy with your service as the loan is going to close and may give you some good leads for future clients.

Ask the borrower if he was happy with the level of service he received throughout the mortgage process. If he says that he is, ask him to give you a few referrals. Ask for a specific number of names: three to five names is a good number to request. Give him one of your business cards and ask him to keep you in mind for future referrals.

The most important thing you can do to build a solid reputation and get a steady stream of referrals is to always conduct yourself in an ethical manner. Recent problems in the subprime mortgage industry can often be traced back to unethical lenders and brokers offering loans to people who cannot possibly afford them. How many of these borrowers will be recommending their broker to a friend? By conducting your business with solid ethics, you will build a reputation as a broker who can be trusted.

Professional referrals are a great source for finding clients. People tend to trust a recommendation from a professional even more than from a friend. This is especially true if they trust the professional giving the recommendation. To generate a steady stream of professional referrals, you need to spend time networking with business people and professionals in your community.

There are several options for meeting professionals in your community. Join some groups in your local community, as some national organizations that may have affiliates in your area include the Rotary Club, Kiwanis, Lions Club, and the Order of Elks. You can find a listing of groups either in your phone book or by searching the Internet. Search for business and community groups with your location to find groups in your area.

Getting involved with the local community can generate referrals. There are several ways to do it that way. You can sponsor a local road or stretch of highway. Signs are posted in many communities with the name of the company that sponsors the road. The cost involves paying for cleanup of local roadways and is not expensive in most communities.

Another way to get involved is to work with a local cleanup or community improvement project. Local parks and recreational associations offer opportunities for businesses to get involved. Donate time or money to the building of a local playground for children. Plaques or other acknowledgements can include the name and location of your business. It is surprising how many people use and refer others to businesses they found through one of these efforts.

Membership in professional organizations can help you generate referrals. Joining organizations for business people is a good way to connect with professionals in your area and gain more referrals. Organizations for women or minorities in business are also good sources for networking. If you are a woman or minority, join the appropriate organization as well as a general organization that is open to all business people.

Organizations vary according to the area in which you live. By doing an Internet search for business organizations and your local city and state, you will find the Web sites for organizations in your area. One that is open to business people in most areas is the chamber of commerce. By attending these meetings on a fairly regular basis, you will have the opportunity to get to know business owners in your area.

One organization that has many benefits is the National Association of Mortgage Brokers (NAMB). This is a national professional organization with state affiliates in all 50 states. These affiliates have a reciprocal agreement with NAMB. When you join your local affiliate chapter, the fee covers both state and national membership. Attending affiliate meetings is a great way to network with other professionals. For more information, visit **www.namb.org**.

Meeting and Connecting With Professionals

When you join the chamber of commerce and other business and professional organizations, there will be events that offer an opportunity for networking. You will need to have a short explanation of who you are and what your responsibilities are. This will help the conversation flow easier when you are meeting people.

Keep your explanation short, but include all pertinent details about your service and what sets you apart from other professionals. How this is done matters. You want to point out your skill without trashing the competition. Trashing the competition turns people off, which is counterproductive when you are trying to gain the confidence of the person you are speaking with and get them to send you referrals.

Do not monopolize the conversation when talking about your service. Ask the other person questions about his business and show an interest. Remember, you are trying to get to know other professionals in a mutually beneficial environment. When you listen, you may learn valuable information. For example, if a business owner is talking about his success and mentions that he is thinking of buying a larger space, he may be in need of a mortgage. If you do not listen, or talk only about you, this opportunity can be missed.

During these events, you will pass out many business cards. You will also be given business cards from the people you met. Make a short note on the back of the card with any pertinent information about the person's business or financial situation. If the person has said he or she will be looking for a mortgage in six months, note this on the card. Make a note of any details you do not want to forget.

In a few weeks, you will contact this person again to follow up on the initial meeting. The notes made on the back of his business card will be valuable during that phone call. When you remember specific details of the conversation, the person will be more likely to have good feelings about you. In addition to asking for referrals, ask how you can help this person. Maybe the firm handles interior design or home security. You may be able to send a few referrals his or her way in addition to gaining some for your business. These mutually beneficial contacts are the most lucrative.

Incentives You Can Offer

Referrals are more effective and less expensive than advertising on the radio or other similar methods. It is a lot less expensive too. One way some brokers use to find referrals and entice companies and individuals to refer potential clients is to offer an incentive. You need to be careful with the incentives you offer to avoid violating RESPA. The United States Department of Housing and Urban Development (HUD) has been cracking down on violations.

There are a variety of kickbacks and referral fees that have been outlawed under RESPA. Fee-splitting between real estate agents and brokers was becoming a costly problem for some borrowers. Kickbacks from lenders to brokers and real estate agents is also addressed in the law. The process often resulted in higher fees at closing and more expensive loans for consumers.

The regulations in RESPA primarily deal with paying compensation for professional referrals. Anything that has value cannot be given to a real estate agent, broker, or lender in exchange for referrals. For example, buying tickets to a concert or a football game for a real estate agent would be considered a violation of RESPA. A scenario like this is considered paying for the referrals and is against the law.

It is possible to offer incentives to borrowers, as long as the incentive is not tied to a specific loan. For example, it is possible to offer discounted fees to the borrower as an incentive to use your service. It is not acceptable to base that discount on using a specific lender, nor is it permitted for the lender to offer the broker something of value to get the loan. As long as any discounted fees or incentives are written in the contract, you are covered from accusations of wrongdoing.

The point of all of this is referrals should be voluntarily given. They are not a commodity to be sold between professionals. This protects the consumer against being pressured to use a lender that is affiliated with an agent or home builder. These types of deals result in increased fees and higher interest rates. All fees and incentives need to be put in the contract to avoid the impression that something is not right with the deal. HUD is cracking down on these illegal practices, and jeopardizing the license you have worked so hard to acquire is not worth going that route.

CHAPTER 9

Finding the Best Deals for Clients

As stated before, a big part of the mortgage broker's time is spent in finding new clients. Without a steady stream of new clients, the broker will not experience success. Once you have found the client, you will want to keep him. The second main part of the broker's job is finding the best deals for his clients. To do this, you need to work with a variety of lenders and build relationships with several lenders.

If you do a great job in finding great deals, this will help you generate leads for future loans. When people have a great experience with a mortgage or refinance, they talk about it with family and friends. Over time, this can generate good word-of-mouth publicity for your business. Since referrals are the best source of leads, you want to cultivate relationships with current clients.

Think of it as a combination of great customer service as well as securing leads and referrals for the future. Finding the best deals for your clients is important both for the client and your future success. The better deals you are able to secure, the more word-of-mouth advertising you will get. This will help with your business reputation and in securing new leads.

Finding Lenders

Finding lenders is not difficult. There are hundreds of lenders offering a wide variety of loan programs for nearly every potential borrower. It is the job of the lender to loan money to borrowers. The mortgage broker is a key resource in the lender doing his job. For this reason, cultivating relationships is beneficial to both the mortgage broker and lender.

There are hundreds of lenders out there, but you could not and should not work with them all. First, it would be nearly impossible to broker loans to hundreds of different companies. Secondly, it is not good for business. You cannot cultivate relationships with hundreds of underwriters and mortgage lenders. It is better to focus on a handful of lenders.

Most mortgage brokers limit their focus to 20 or fewer companies. This gives a good selection of loan programs for clients, while allowing the broker to build relationships with lenders. As you send loans to these lenders, you will get to know them and get updates on new programs being offered.

You will continue to find new lenders to work with throughout your career as a mortgage broker. Mortgage companies have representatives that work with brokers to bring more loans to the lender. These representatives will contact you from time to time to let you know about new programs being offered to borrowers.

As you find new lenders with good programs for your clients, you can add them to your list. Work to get to know these new lenders, while cultivating your relationships with the others you have been working with. This will give you a steady stream of loan options to offer your clients.

Taking the time to find the best deals for your clients will result in more referrals. Word of mouth is very powerful advertising. When friends, family members, and business associates of your clients hear about the great deals you are putting together, they will want to use your service for their mortgage needs. This will result in more referrals that lead to more loan closings.

Mortgage Magazines

Every mortgage broker should at least read some mortgage magazines every month. In general, you should subscribe to at least one, if not more. There are several benefits to subscribing to these magazines. One benefit is in finding lenders, as mortgage companies often advertise in magazines to reach brokers and other professionals. You can find lenders in the advertisements or classified section of these magazines.

There is an even bigger benefit to subscribing to magazines about the mortgage industry: your continuing education. Both borrowers and lenders prefer a mortgage broker with knowledge of the industry. Knowledge of the changes in the mortgage industry and the current condition of the real estate and mortgage markets are helpful to your success as a mortgage broker.

It is important to keep abreast of changes in the industry. This will not only help you stay current, but will improve your credibility. When potential clients call you on the phone, they will be impressed by your knowledge of the industry and of changes that are on the horizon. This enhances your image as a successful professional and can bring you more business and referrals from clients.

Popular Mortgage Magazines

Scotsman Guide, **www.scotsmanguide.com** – This is a leading publication for comparing loan programs from different lenders. Both the magazine and Web site offer information on loan programs, credit, and a variety of other issues and topics. The best part is that this publication is available free of charge. Sign up for a free subscription on the magazine's Web site.

The Mortgage Chronicle, **www.mortgagechronicle.com** – This is another free publication that is a valuable resource for any professional working in the mortgage industry. The Web site offers a wide range of articles, information, mortgage leads, employment, and information about lenders and loan programs.

Mortgage Banking magazine, **www.mortgagebankingmagazine.com** – This magazine provides in-depth coverage into all aspects of the mortgage and real estate finance industries. It is published by the Mortgage Bankers Association and is read by mortgage brokers, mortgage bankers, and executives in the mortgage industry.

Broker magazine, **www.brokermagazine.com** – This is a monthly publication that is geared toward mortgage brokers. Each month, a wide variety of topics related to both residential and commercial mortgages, as well as features and information about the industry, keep brokers up to date and informed.

Mortgage Originator, **www.mortgageoriginator.com** – This magazine covers topics such as industry news, strategies, management, technology, and more. Many articles are also available on the Web site.

National Mortgage News, **www.nationalmortgagenews.com** – This is a weekly publication with updated news and information related to the mortgage industry. There are daily news briefings on the Web site and an option for free mortgage headlines sent to your inbox. As a subscriber to this publication, the broker will have access to additional information and premium content on the magazine's Web site.

National Mortgage Broker Magazine, **www.nambmagazine.com** – This is the official magazine of the National Association of Mortgage Brokers (NAMB). The goal of the publication is to offer features, new information, and regular columns to keep their subscribers up to date with changes in the industry.

Professional Organizations

Professional organizations are another great way to find and connect with lenders and other professionals in the mortgage industry. This can be done in person through local and state affiliates or online.

The National Association of Mortgage Brokers, **www.namb.org** – This is the leading professional association for mortgage brokers. The NAMB has affiliate organizations in each state. Members join the state affiliate and part of those dues entitle the broker to membership in the national organization as well.

National Association of Mortgage Professionals, **www.namp.org**– This organization is open to all people working in the mortgage industry. As a member of this organization, the broker is seen as a trusted professional. Brokers and other mortgage professionals can benefit from the information and resources on the Web site. To access this area, you must be a member of NAMP. You can subscribe to a monthly newsletter on the Web site as well.

The National Organization of Professional Mortgage Women, **www.napmw.org** – NAPMW was founded in 1964 to promote women in the mortgage lending profession. The organization is open for membership to both women and men. The organization offers continuing education, networking opportunities, and information.

Mortgage Bankers Association, **www.mortgagebankers.org** – This is an organization that is open to all professionals in the real estate finance industry. Members include mortgage brokers, mortgage companies, commercial banks, and other professionals in the mortgage lending industry.

Building Relationships With Lenders

Cultivating relationships with lenders is worth your time. The best way to do this is to use the lender and get to know the people that work for that company. One way to do this is to send loans to the lender consistently. When you send loans to the same company, you will be speaking to the same people. Take advantage of this opportunity to get to know these lenders.

Be pleasant in your transactions with the people you are dealing with at the mortgage companies. Exchange pleasant comments and make a bit of small talk to break the ice. Underwriters are used to dealing with cranky brokers and borrowers. They appreciate a polite and friendly broker. In fact, many would prefer to work with that broker over the others. Be the broker the lender likes to work with. Your calls will be returned faster.

Be sure the majority of the loans you send are considered to be a good risk. Lenders want to offer loans to customers that are considered to be safe in terms of risk. When you send a fairly consistent supply of good-risk loan applications to the lender, you will become known as a reliable broker and the lender will want to cultivate a relationship with you.

A big benefit of cultivating relationships is help with loan approval. While you want the majority of the files you send to the lender to be in the good-risk category, this will not always be the case. From time to time, you will send a file that is borderline in terms of risk. If you have built a solid reputation with the lender, the underwriter will be more willing to work with you and the borrower. Since you have built a relationship with the company, they will trust your judgment more.

It will take time to build a relationship with the lender, but it is worth the effort involved. In the end, the best way to build your reputation with the lender is to send quality loans their way on a fairly consistent basis. The more you work with the lender and get to know the people, the easier time you will have with your loans.

Keeping Borrowers and Lenders Happy

As a mortgage broker, you will need to learn to keep both the borrower and the lender happy throughout the loan application and closing processes. This can be a fine line to walk since each party has different objectives in the loan process. With some planning and foresight, you will be able to keep both parties happy and ensure a smooth transaction.

Goals of the Borrower

Although the goals can differ from borrower to borrower, most have the same basic objective: to get the best deal possible on a mortgage. Some will want to do this with as little money down as possible; others will have a large down payment from the sale of another property and will not be concerned about lowering the down payment requirements.

As a mortgage broker, it is your job to determine the goals of your client and help them meet those goals to the best of your ability. Many borrowers do not have much knowledge about home mortgages. It will be your role to educate the borrower about the loan products that are available and help him select the best one to meet his needs.

The first step is to sit down with the clients and discuss their financial situation. Once you have determined their income and expenses, you will be able to help them find a loan with payments they can afford to make. You will be able to determine which loan programs they will qualify for, which will allow you to focus your energies on getting them the best loan to fit their circumstances and long-term financial goals.

Goals of the Lender

The goal of the lender is to loan money for mortgages, second mortgages, and home equity lines of credit. The lender has money to lend. They like to work with mortgage brokers because brokers will bring them borrowers. The lender may not attract these borrowers without the help of a broker. This increases the number of loans the lender is able to secure.

While lenders are looking to loan money, that does not mean they will take any loan. They want borrowers that are considered a good risk. This decreases the likelihood that the borrower will default on the loan. Lenders want to loan money to people that they feel will be able to maintain the payments and keep the loan current.

The best way to keep the lender happy is to supply a steady stream of good quality loans. Take the time to anticipate the underwriter's questions. When you submit the application package, include supporting documentation in the form of financial records. Letters explaining periods of poor credit or the income of the self-employed borrower can and should be included in the package. When you cover your bases and answer questions before they are asked, the loan approval process will be faster and smoother.

Not all of the applications a mortgage broker sends will fit this description. Some loans are tougher than others. A certain percentage will be borrowers with less-than-perfect credit. Another percentage will have issues with employment and showing a steady income, which are often self-employed borrowers. Some will have an uneven salary history. This is typical with seasonal work, such as contractors.

A benefit of building a good rapport with the lender will be seen in your ability to get these less-than-perfect loans approved. If you send the lender mostly borrowers that are considered to be a good risk, the lender will begin to trust your judgment. This can help you with the more difficult loans. Since you know the borrower's situation better than the lender, you can offer information to clarify the credit or income issues. Since the lender knows you to be a quality professional, they will be more likely to trust your judgment.

Finding a Balance to Keep Both Happy

A skilled and successful mortgage broker is able to keep both the borrower and the lender happy throughout the transaction. There will be times when this is not possible. Maybe despite your best efforts a client is denied a mortgage. Occasionally, a file will be incomplete and the underwriter will contact you for more information. These situations are inevitable, but try to make the occurrences as rare as possible.

The best way to do this is with good communication. Communicate with both the borrower and the lender throughout the process. Begin with your first meeting with the borrower. Have a conversation about his or her income, employment, and credit history. Be sure the borrower understands that honesty is important. Dishonesty on a mortgage application is likely to be discovered, which can result in denial of the loan.

Pull the client's credit report for that first meeting, if at all possible. If a couple is looking for a mortgage, pull the credit report for each of them. Go over the credit report with the clients. You will be able to see if the problem with slow payments was a temporary thing or an ongoing issue. This will give you an understanding of their situation and help you find the best program to fit their needs.

You may be able to make suggestions to help the borrower increase the likelihood of approval. If there are a lot of small outstanding balances you know the lender will want paid off, tell the borrower. The advance notice can help the borrower gain approval. He can pay off some of the items in his credit report. While the credit score will remain lower, it looks better if some of the older outstanding items are paid off.

This will keep the lender happy at the same time. The lender likes to see bills getting paid and explanations for periods of slow credit. They like to see information that clarifies questions regarding income or the business of a self-employed borrower. When you take the time to get all these things in order prior to sending the loan package to the underwriter, the lender will be happy with your service.

CHAPTER

10

Putting Together a Loan Package

A large portion of the mortgage broker's time is spent in putting together loan packages for lender approval. You will work with the borrower to gather necessary documentation and complete the loan application. This is then submitted to the lender for approval. In the beginning, this will feel like a daunting task. Once you become familiar with the process, it will become much easier.

Credit Reports and Scores

One of the first things you will do when putting together a loan package is to pull the borrower's credit report. If it is a couple, you will need to pull the credit report of both borrowers. There are three credit reporting companies in the United States, Equifax, TransUnion, and Experian. A credit report must be obtained from each of the three companies to give a good picture of the borrower's credit rating.

It is important for all mortgage brokers to understand credit reports and how they are scored. This is particularly true for brokers dealing with subprime lenders and borrowers with less-than-perfect credit. These lenders have programs designed for borrowers with credit issues. Often, these programs are linked to specific requirements regarding late payments and account history information.

The credit report contains information reported to the credit bureau by financial institutions that have done business with your borrower. Information is listed about the accounts including the type of loan, dates, and payments, and whether those payments were received on time or not. The amount of available credit and account balances are also listed for each entry in the report.

One thing the lender will look at is the payment history of the borrower. Next to the information about the amount owed will be numbers showing how many times the borrower was late. Late payments are classified as 30+, 60+, 90+, or 120+, showing how late the payment was received and how many times payments have been received that late. For example, a 2 under 30+ shows that the account was paid more than 30 days after the due date on two occasions. This information tells lenders how the client has paid debts in the past, which is believed to be a good indication of how the borrower will pay bills in the future.

The following section on the credit report is for public records. This will show any judgments against the borrower. Foreclosures and bankruptcy are also listed in this section. The information listed in this section can significantly bring down a credit score, specifically bankruptcy or a previous foreclosure.

The next section of the credit report is where inquiries are listed. This includes information about companies that have looked at the borrower's credit report. Lenders see a large number of inquires as a bad sign. This may signal that the borrower is in danger of becoming financially overextended in the coming months or years. It is best if inquires are kept to a minimum.

However, not all inquires are bad. For example, if the borrower is in the market for a mortgage and the underwriter sees that three mortgage companies have pulled the credit report, this will not hurt the borrower. This is seen as one event, rather than three. Obviously the borrower is applying for one mortgage, not three. Lenders hate a long list of various companies, including mortgage companies, car dealers, and credit card companies. For this reason, most brokers advise clients not to apply for loans or buy cars when applying for a mortgage.

Helping Borrowers Improve Their Scores

Technically, you are not a credit counselor. Assisting borrowers to improve their credit scores is not your primary job, but it is beneficial to both you and the borrower. As the borrower increases his or her credit score, they will qualify for a better loan program. In some cases, the borrower may take a subprime, adjustable rate mortgage due to low credit scores. If you help them to improve their scores, they will be able to qualify for a better interest rate in a year or two.

When that time comes, they will be more likely to come back to you for help in finding a better loan. As a mortgage broker, you always should have your eye on your future business and building good relations with your clients. Offering information on improving credit scores when meeting with clients and in literature sent via mail, e-mail, or listed on your Web site is a good way to help your clients and build good will for the future. This can translate into the client coming back to you for future mortgage needs as well as referring friends to you for their mortgage needs.

To help borrowers increase their scores, you need to understand how credit scoring works. Credit scores are also known as FICO scores. This comes from the company that calculates these scores, the Fair Isaac Corporation. FICO uses complicated calculations to arrive at a credit score between 300 and 800. Few borrowers have a perfect credit score or a score as low as 300. The average score in America is around 650.

The FICO system assigns points based on several factors. Points can be gained for paying on time, having low balances compared to available credit, and the length of time the borrower has held the account. Points are lost on the credit score for late payments and having balances over the credit limit.

The score looks at all these factors over a period of the previous two years. This gives a more long-term picture of the person's credit history than looking at a shorter period of time. Items can remain on the credit report for up to seven years and do continue to affect the score, but the main focus is on the last two.

The payment history makes up 38 percent of the credit score. This is how the borrower pays his bills. A credit report with on-time payments on all accounts will have a higher score than a report reflecting lateness in paying bills. A few late payments on one account will have less of an effect than several accounts showing multiple late payments.

Another important factor in calculating the credit score is the amount of credit available to the borrower. This is the credit available compared to the amount of money owed on accounts. In other words, the credit limit on credit cards and lines of credit compared with the balances on these accounts. The score will be higher when there is more available credit than when all accounts are at the maximum credit line.

The best-case scenario for the borrower is to keep the balances at no more than 30 percent of available credit. This leaves 70 percent of the maximum credit available to the borrower. For example, on a credit card with a limit of $10,000, the borrower should keep the outstanding balance at no more than $3,000. This leaves $7,000 of available credit. Lenders like to see that the borrower is not maxed out financially. It is seen as an indication of the ability to manage money and pay bills.

Despite the advertising by credit counseling companies, the best way to improve a credit score is to pay bills on time and give it some time. Credit scores will not increase significantly in a short period of time. However, as the borrower makes timely payments over a period of months, the score will increase.

There are other ways to improve the score. One is to look at the report for mistakes or old items. The system is far from perfect and the majority of borrowers have at least one mistake on their credit reports. These items can be disputed and must be removed from the credit report.

The public records section is one area where the borrower should focus. There is nothing that can be done about foreclosures or bankruptcies if they are recent. But there may be other items listed in this section that can be rectified. The borrower can clear up any liens or judgments that are listed here to help bring up the score.

The old advice for credit reports was to close out accounts that are not currently being used. This may not be the best advice. Since a portion of the credit score focuses on the amount of available credit compared with outstanding balances, accounts that are open but have zero balances can help raise the score. Closing these accounts could actually make the score drop and your clients definitely do not want a lower score.

Application Process

The amount of money the borrower can use as a down payment is an important consideration in securing a mortgage loan. The lender's requirements regarding a down payment will vary according to several factors. The loan-to-value ratio is one factor that will make a difference in how much the lender wants the borrower to put down.

The borrower's debt-to-income ratio is another factor. This is the amount of money the borrower makes each month compared with the expenses going out. Each lender and loan program has slightly different requirements for debt to income. The lower the borrower's debt-to-income ratio, the better for the borrower in terms of being approved for a mortgage.

There are benefits to putting down more money on a home mortgage. With a larger down payment, the monthly payment on the loan will be lower. This may be important for the debt-to-income ratio. If the loan amount is too high for the ratio they want, the borrower may be asked to put more money down to bring down the amount of the loan. If the loan is granted, the interest rate may be higher.

One way some borrowers get around this is to take a piggyback loan. This is a smaller second mortgage to cover the down payment. The borrower takes a first mortgage for the maximum amount that the lender will allow. A smaller second mortgage is then taken for the balance of the purchase price. The interest rate on the second mortgage will be higher, but the loan balance will be smaller.

There are a few drawbacks to taking a piggyback loan. One is that there will be less equity in the home. The equity will grow at a slower rate until after the second mortgage is paid off. Until that time, the borrower will not be able to take a second mortgage or home equity line of credit for other things.

With two loans, it is easier for the borrower to become overextended financially. This can result in a greater risk that the borrower will default on the loan. This puts the property at risk of foreclosure. If a client is interested in using a piggyback loan to bridge the gap between financing and the purchase price of the home, be sure he can comfortably afford the payments.

The type of loan will also have an impact on how much money the borrower is asked to put down on the mortgage. Some loan programs ask for a larger down payment. Conventional mortgages often require larger down payments, such as 10 or 20 percent of the total sale price of the home. Other programs offer loans with a much smaller down payment. FHA loans require a down payment of between 3 and 5 percent. VA loans require no down payment.

Underwriters

When the loan package is complete, you will send it to the lender. The underwriter's job is to make the decision on approval or denial on behalf of the lender. The underwriter will look at the application package and the financial documents provided when making a decision on the loan. If information is missing or additional documentation is needed, the underwriter will call you to ask for it.

You will need to go back to your client and request the missing information. This can make the approval process take longer. To keep the ball rolling, you need to anticipate the underwriter's questions and send everything that is needed. Not only will this speed the approval process, but it will endear you to the underwriter. Consistently sending complete packages and anticipating their questions is a great way to build relationships.

The borrower will also benefit from your foresight. The approval and closing of the loan will go much more smoothly when you are well prepared, which also increases the likelihood of an approval. When clients have a good experience and everything goes smoothly, the client is more likely to give you referrals and recommend your service to friends, family, and coworkers.

Putting together a loan application, sending it to the underwriter, and praying for an approval is not the way to go to business. By the time the application is submitted, you should feel confident that it will be approved. The best way to do this is to understand the guidelines for that lender. If it is a conventional mortgage, be sure the borrower meets the guidelines set forth by Fannie Mae and Freddie Mac.

Every mortgage broker should be familiar with these guidelines. However, all loans do not conform to the guidelines of Fannie Mae and Freddie Mac. Therefore, you will need to learn about the specific loan products that the lenders are offering. When sending an application package, be sure the borrower's situation fits the product. If not, an approval is less likely.

From time to time, lenders will send you information about new loan programs that they are offering. Take the time to read the information carefully to be sure you understand the requirements for each type of loan. If you have any questions, this is the time to ask, because you do not want to be peppering them with questions after you have sent an application for approval. When you receive the information, call with any questions. This way you will be sure to understand the guidelines and will send complete packages that are ready for approval.

Guidelines are subject to change. The guidelines for a lender today are most likely not the same as last year. It is your job to stay abreast of any changes. Stay current with changes to the guidelines for conforming loans and read updates from various lenders carefully. In addition, spend time reading about the mortgage industry and note any changes that are occurring. Think of this as part of your continuing education as a mortgage broker.

Appraiser

An appraisal will be required for mortgage loans. The appraisal determines the market value of the house and, as a result, the amount that the lender will finance. The appraisal will be conducted by a professional appraiser who is approved by the mortgage company. This will be done early in the process to be sure that the amount the borrower wants to finance will work with the value of the home. The fee for this service varies, but is generally between $300 and $400.

The appraiser will inspect the home on the inside and the outside. He or she will take measurements of the outside of the home, property, and the interior of the home. Each room will be measured to determine the total square footage of living area. The size and condition of the home are big factors in the property value.

The other major factor that influences the value of the property is the value of the properties in the surrounding area. The appraiser determines this by using comparables. These are properties that have been sold in the same area as the home that will be mortgaged. The homes will be of comparable size to the home being financed. The lender wants to see comparable properties that have sold within the last six months.

Parts of an Appraisal Report

There are a few different formats used for appraisal reports, depending on the purpose and the requirements of the lenders. Most lenders require that the same items be shown on the appraisal report for the purposes of securing financing. There is a standard form used by the majority of lenders in the United States, which is called the Uniform Residential Appraisal Report (URAR). This report can be found online at **www.efanniemae.com/sf/formsdocs/forms/pdf/sellingtrans/1004.pdf.**

Sections of the URAR

Subject: This section lists basic information about the property being appraised. The address, names of the owner and borrower, and a complete legal description of the property are included in this section.

Contract: In this section, the information related to the sales contract is listed.

Neighborhood: This section contains information on the neighborhood where the home is located. The location, growth, property values, and information on supply and demand for real estate in the area are categorized by checklist. A written description of the neighborhood and general market conditions in the area is required on the URAR form.

Site: A variety of information is listed in this section, including the size and shape of the property. Information regarding access to utilities and the zoning category of the property is included here. If the home is in a FEMA-designated flood zone, this is listed in this section of the URAR.

Improvements: This section includes information about the physical structure. The age of the home and current condition is described here. Improvements made to the home since original construction and the materials used in those improvements are listed. In some cases, this section can increase or decrease the appraised value, depending on the condition of the property and renovations completed.

Sales Comparison: This is the area of the appraisal report where comparables are listed. A grid is completed to show the location of the property being appraised in relation to other homes recently sold in the area. Three comparables are used in this section of the form. The selling price of these homes will influence the appraised value of the property.

There are three different approaches to appraising property. For the purposes of Fannie Mae and most other lending institutions, the sales comparison approach is the only one required. The two other approaches are the cost approach and income approach. There is space on the URAR form for these two approaches where the appraiser enters relevant information.

The sales comparison approach is the method required by Fannie Mae and preferred by nearly all residential lenders. This method examines the property and features of that property. The selling price of similar properties is then used to help determine the value. Often, exact comparables cannot be found. The price on the appraisal is adjusted to reflect the differences.

The cost approach uses the cost of reproducing the structure to estimate the value of the property. The formula involves calculating the value of the property and the depreciated value of improvements made to the property. This method is most reliable when used with newer homes. When older homes are used, the information is not as reliable due to several factors. The improvements are often more difficult to calculate as well as the replacement cost.

The income approach is not generally used for residential properties. This approach is used to value properties which will be used for commercial or investment purposes. The income approach uses the net operating income, gross potential income, and operating expenses in calculations to determine the value of the property.

The calculations and figures used will be determined by the type of property and the amount of income the property would produce. If you work strictly on residential loans, you may never see this method. Commercial brokers will see this approach used for commercial properties, particularly large projects.

The appraisal report is generally sent to the lender when it is complete. In some cases, a copy is sent to the mortgage broker and then forwarded to the lender. From time to time a borrower may ask for a copy. The borrower can always request a copy of the appraisal from the lender.

Truth in Lending

The Truth in Lending Act is a federal law that was passed in 1968 as part of the Consumer Credit Protection Act. The purpose of the law is to protect borrowers from fraud by requiring disclosure of the costs involved in taking a mortgage. According to the law, the lender must present the borrower with a statement that estimates the costs and percentage rate within three days of the application. At this point, these will be estimates.

The Good Faith Estimate is just an estimate of the closing costs, as the actual costs will be different. The final costs and interest rate will be listed in the Uniform Settlement Statement. This document will give the borrower the exact costs related to closing on the loan. The Uniform Settlement Statement is available one business day before closing.

The Truth in Lending statement will have information on the interest rate and the annual percentage rate (APR). This is often confusing for borrowers to understand. They often see the APR and notice it is higher than the rate quoted for the loan. Your phone will ring shortly after they see that information. You will be asked to explain the discrepancy.

The APR includes the total yield on the loan. The figure includes the origination fees and discount points. The interest rate of the loan is located farther down on the form. Other information on the Truth in Lending statement includes the finance charges and the total amount of payments the borrower will pay over the life of the loan. Information about the term of the loan, number of payments, monthly payment, and due date are also included on this form.

The Truth in Lending act gives borrowers a right of rescission. The borrower has three days to change his mind with certain home equity loans and second mortgages. The right of rescission does not apply to a home loan to purchase a home. It does apply to any refinancing, second mortgage, home equity loan, or home equity line of credit that is secured with the borrower's home.

If the borrower is refinancing with the same lender, there is no right of rescission. As long as the refinance or second mortgage is with a different lender, the borrower will have three days to change his mind. The right of rescission only applies when the property is the borrower's primary residence. It does not apply to a vacation home, rental home, or investment property.

Under the right of rescission, the borrower can change his mind within three days of closing with no questions asked. To exercise the right, the borrower must notify the lender in writing that he wishes to use his right of rescission and cancel the loan. The lender has 20 days from that date to refund any fees paid by the borrower and give up its claim on the property.

Title Company

All lenders require borrowers to purchase title insurance prior to closing. The title insurance is a bit different than any other insurance policy. Most insurance is purchased to protect the insured against unforeseen events that can occur in the future, such as a car accident or fire in the home. Title insurance protects against mistakes in the past. For example, the title search showed a clear title, but there was a lien against the property. The insurance protects the borrower and the lender from loss in the event of such a mistake.

The title company will do a title search and examine public records to be sure that:

- There are no liens on the property
- The seller is the legal owner of the property being sold
- There are no mortgages or judgments against the property
- There are no easements or other restrictions tied to the property
- Property taxes are paid up to date

In many real estate transactions involving the sale of a home, the buyer will put down a deposit, also known as earnest money. These funds are deposited in escrow with the title company. The funds are held by the title company until the closing of the sale. At that time, the money held in escrow as earnest money is applied toward the down payment of the borrower.

The title company prepares the deed and coordinates the documents required at closing. Settlements often take place in the office of the title company, but it may take place in a lawyer's office. When it comes time to close, a representative from the title company will handle the closing. They will make sure that all documents are signed and everything is completed as required by law.

The title company representative will explain the documents to the borrower before signing. They will answer questions about each document and offer clarification if the borrower does not understand a particular document or figure. The title company is responsible for the money that changes hands during the transaction. If the borrower is doing a refinance with cash-out, the title company will hold the check for the three day rescission period. At that time, they will get it to the borrower.

After settlement, the title company will submit the documents to be recorded legally. The documents are then returned to the title company after they have been recorded. The title company will send these documents to the lender or borrower, depending on the requirements of the loan agreement.

CHAPTER 11

Private Mortgage Segment

For most mortgage brokers, a large portion of their business comes from the private mortgage segment. These are mortgages for noncommercial real estate properties. To be successful as a broker, you will need to have knowledge of the various types of loan programs available in the private mortgage segment of the industry.

Freddie Mac

The Federal Home Loan Mortgage Corporation, also known as Freddie Mac, was founded in 1970. The purpose was to expand the secondary mortgage market. This made getting a mortgage easier for many people and generated more money available for the home lending industry.

Freddie Mac is a private corporation that is stockholder owned. It is sponsored by the U.S. government, but it receives no governmental funding. Freddie Mac purchases mortgage loans on the secondary mortgage market. These loans are then pooled and sold as mortgage-backed securities.

This process generates more money, which is then available to make new loans for other borrowers. Money continues to be available for future new home purchases, which makes it possible for more people to realize the dream of home ownership.

Freddie Mac charges investors a guarantee fee on the loans in the mortgage-backed security bonds. This fee is in exchange for Freddie Mac assuming the risk of the borrower defaulting on a loan. The guarantee is that the principal and interest on the loan will be paid, even if the borrower defaults.

Fannie Mae

The Federal National Mortgage Association, or Fannie Mae, is a private corporation similar to Freddie Mac. Fannie Mae is older than Freddie Mac and was originally a government agency. It was founded under Franklin Delano Roosevelt in 1938 to help generate funds for the private mortgage market.

Fannie Mae became a private corporation in 1968. The corporation works in the same way as Freddie Mac; purchasing loans and selling them as mortgage-backed securities. Fannie Mae had the monopoly on the secondary mortgage market for over 30 years. Freddie Mac was founded to offer more competition and generate more money for mortgage lending. Fannie Mae and Freddie Mac set the standards for conforming loans in the mortgage industry.

Ginnie Mae

The Government National Mortgage Association, or Ginnie Mae, works in a different way than Freddie Mac and Fannie Mae. This corporation is owned by the United States government under the Department of Housing and Urban Development (HUD).

Like the other entities, Ginnie Mae provides guarantees on the mortgage-backed securities for federally guaranteed loans. The difference is that loans under Ginnie Mac are guaranteed by the United States government. These include loans from the Department of Veterans Affairs, Federal Housing Administration, and Rural Housing Service. These are the only mortgage-backed securities that are guaranteed by the government.

Conforming Loans

Conforming loans conform to the standards set by Freddie Mac and Fannie Mae. All other loans are considered nonconforming. The two entities worked together to create the standards for conforming loans. All loans purchased by these entities and resold as mortgage-backed securities are conforming loans.

Requirements for Conforming Loans

The borrower must have excellent credit to qualify for a conforming loan. This is done to minimize the risk, since the entities are guaranteeing payment of the loans they purchase and sell as mortgage-backed securities. The criterion can vary, but a minimum credit score of 680 is pretty standard for conforming loans. Also:

- The loan must be the primary mortgage and not a second mortgage.
- Employment must be verified for the past two years.

- More documentation is required for conforming loans, including bank statements to show assets.
- The debt-to-income and loan-to-value ratio guidelines are more stringent for conforming loans.
- There are limits on the size of a conforming loan. This limit varies according to the housing market. The mean home price is used in determining the annual loan limits.

The following table contains the loan limits for conforming loans for 2007:

Property Type	Loan Limit
Single Family	**$417,000**
2 Unit	$533,850
3 Unit	$645,300
4 Unit	$801,950

The biggest benefit to conforming loans is the interest rate. The rate is lower for conforming loans than for loans that do not conform to the requirements of Freddie Mac and Fannie Mae. The interest rate is about one-half of 1 percent lower than a similar nonconforming loan.

Nonconforming Loans

Nonconforming loans are loans that do not conform to the guidelines set by Freddie Mac and Fannie Mae. There are several reasons a loan may not conform to the requirements. One is the size of the loan. If the loan amount is higher than the limit set by Freddie Mac and Fannie Mae, it is known as a jumbo loan.

Some borrowers will take a second mortgage to cover the difference between the loan limit for a conforming loan and the purchase price of the house. This saves money for the borrower since the interest rate for jumbo loans is higher. For example, the borrower may take a conforming loan for the limit allowed. A second mortgage would then be taken for the difference. The interest rate on the second mortgage will be higher, but the loan amount will be smaller. This method can save a significant amount of money.

The credit history of the borrower is another reason for a nonconforming loan. If the credit score is below the limit set by Freddie Mac and Fannie Mae, the borrower will not qualify for a conforming loan. In most cases, the borrower will still be able to secure financing for the purchase. This is done on the subprime mortgage market.

The rate for nonconforming loans is generally higher than for a comparable conforming loan. Mortgage brokers often deal with nonconforming loans and shop around for the best terms and rate for the borrower. For many borrowers, it is easier for them to qualify for these loans than for a standard conforming loan.

Fixed vs. Adjustable Mortgages

There are two basic types of mortgages, fixed or adjustable interest rates. Fixed-rate mortgages have one interest rate for the life of the loan. Adjustable-rate mortgages (ARMs) have an interest rate that fluctuates based on index rates. There are pros and cons to both fixed and adjustable rates. The best scenario for the client will depend on a few factors.

Fixed-Rate Mortgages

The interest rate on a fixed-rate mortgage does not change. The payment will remain the same from the first month to the last. The amount of that payment that goes toward the principal on the loan will vary. In the early years, more of each payment goes toward the interest. As the loan matures, more of each payment is put toward the principal on the loan.

The term of fixed-rate mortgages varies. The 30-year loan remains the most common, but there are 15- and 20-year options as well. The longer the term of the loan, the lower the amount of the monthly payment. If the borrower can afford the higher payment, a 15- or 20-year loan will result in a lot less money paid in interest over the life of the loan. Another benefit is that the loan will be paid off faster.

Some fixed-rate mortgages offer a biweekly payment option. The borrower pays half the monthly payment every two weeks. This results in an additional monthly mortgage payment being made by the end of the year. This additional money goes directly to the principal. An advantage of this for the borrower is the loan can be paid off about ten years faster with that additional principal.

The biweekly payment option may be good for some borrowers, if they can afford the payment schedule. If not, the same benefit can be had by sending in extra principal payments when possible. Check the requirements for additional principal payments when comparing loans from different lenders. In most fixed-rate mortgages, the additional money can be sent with the regular monthly payment.

There are certain situations in which a fixed-rate loan is most likely the best choice for the borrower. If the borrower can afford the monthly payment with a higher fixed rate and does not want to risk rising interest rates or having to refinance later, a fixed rate is probably the best bet. When interest rates are low or are predicted to increase in the near future, fixed-rate mortgages are a good choice.

If the borrower plans to live in the home for many years to come, a fixed rate may be a good choice. Of course, the borrower could take the lower teaser rate on the ARM and then refinance, but some borrowers do not want that hassle. In this case, starting off with a fixed rate is the best bet. Again, this is particularly true when the interest rates are low.

Advantages of a fixed rate:

- The payment remains the same every month.
- The borrower does not have to worry about payments skyrocketing if interest rates go up.
- Financial planning and budgeting are easier when payment amounts are fixed.

Disadvantages of a fixed rate:

- The interest rate on fixed-rate mortgages tends to be higher than the teaser rates offered on ARMs.
- There are various fees included in these loans. The fees charged vary from lender to lender, so more care is needed in comparing loan programs.

Adjustable-Rate Mortgages

Adjustable-rate mortgages have a variable interest rate. This means the interest rate at the time of closing will not be the rate for the life of the loan. The interest rate paid on the loan will rise and fall according to whatever index the lender is using. Some of the common indexes used to set the rates for ARMs include the prime interest rate, Cost of Funds index, or the London Interbank Offered Rate (LIBOR).

Often there will be an initial period of time when the interest rate will remain the same. This can be from one to seven years, depending on the loan and the lender. For this period of time, the lower initial interest rate will remain in effect. After this initial time period, the rate changes to an adjustable rate and the payment will change.

Recently, these loans have been getting attention in the media. The skyrocketing monthly payments associated with some of these mortgages are thought to be a contributing factor to the increased rate of foreclosures in the United States. The payments rise sharply and the borrower ends up defaulting on the loan.

There are ways to help avoid this problem. For borrowers interested in adjustable-rate mortgages, look for loans with caps that restrict the amount interest rates can increase during each adjustment period. Some loans have a cap on how much the payment can increase, but not the interest rate. These are also known as negative amortization loans.

The cap on the payment means the payment can only increase a certain amount during each adjustment period, also known as the adjustment frequency. This helps keep the payment lower, but there is a downside to these loans. The difference in the increase in the interest rate and the cap on the payment is added to the balance of the loan. In some cases, the balance actually increases as the borrower makes payments on the loan.

The danger for the borrower in this scenario is that the amount of money owed on the house is increasing rather than decreasing as payments are made. This can be bad if the borrower wants to refinance, because there is less equity in the home. If the borrower intends to sell, it will increase the amount of money required to satisfy the mortgage and decrease the profit the borrower would make when selling the home.

Advantages of an adjustable rate:

- The initial interest rate is lower than fixed rate loans.
- The monthly payment will be lower in the initial loan period.
- It may be easier for the borrower to qualify for the loan, since the payment is lower in the beginning.
- If interest rates decline, the payment will drop.

Disadvantages of an adjustable rate:

- After the initial period, the interest rate will change. This can result in much higher payments.
- If interest rates go up, the payment goes up too.
- If property values decline or the borrower's credit is not

great, it can be difficult to refinance, especially if payments get behind.

- The possibility of negative amortization.

Interest-Only Loans

Interest-only loans are a type of mortgage where the borrower is making payments on only the interest. None of the monthly payment is applied to the principal. These loans are available in either fixed or adjustable rate mortgages. The loan remains interest only for a certain number of years, usually either five or ten. At that time, the loan becomes an amortized mortgage and the new payment reflects both interest and principal payments.

The benefit of interest-only loans is the lower monthly payment. Because the borrower is only repaying the interest, the payment is lower. There is a lot of risk associated with interest-only loans. If there is a drop in the property value, the borrower can end up owing more than what the house is worth.

The payments can still skyrocket if the loan is an ARM. The interest-only time period is not necessarily the same as the time period for the initial interest rate. For example, an ARM can have a ten-year interest-only option and only a one-year time period before the interest rate on the loan becomes adjustable. After this time period, the payment can increase.

As interest rates for home mortgages increase, the payment on the interest-only loan can go up significantly. There is still no money being applied to the principal of the loan. This situation can make refinancing out of the loan more difficult, particularly if home prices are dropping. In addition, it can make it nearly impossible for many borrowers to add extra money to the principal.

Borrowers have the option of adding additional principal payments, if desired, during the interest-only period of the loan. If the borrower has extra money or wants to use part of his income tax return to pay down some of the principal, this can be done. It may be a good idea to suggest this to clients that take an interest-only loan. Any additional principal payments can help reduce the risk of the loan getting bigger than the value of the property.

The interest rate on an interest-only loan is generally not lower. The rate is often a little higher than a similar traditional loan. The reason for this is the additional risk to the lender. There is a higher chance of default on an interest-only mortgage. Often the reason for this is rising interest rates and falling property values.

There are some situations in which an interest-only loan may make sense. If the borrower is self-employed in a seasonal line of work that results in more money at certain times of the year, an interest-only loan may be a good thing. The borrower can pay more money in the months when he is earning more and that money will be applied toward the principal. In the leaner months, he can enjoy the lower payments of interest only.

If the borrower earns bonuses at certain intervals during the year and plans to put this money toward the principal, an interest-only loan may be the best choice. He can pay only the interest each month and add additional principal payments in the months when he earns a bonus. In both of these scenarios, the borrower would be making additional principal payments.

Sometimes a borrower anticipates a large salary increase within a few years after purchasing a home. Maybe the borrower is in medical school or another program that will result in a high-paying job in the fairly near future. The borrower can get through school with the lower payments and then either refinance or pay additional principal when he is earning more money.

Graduated-Payment Mortgage

A graduated-payment mortgage is a type of mortgage in which the payments are initially low and get higher over time. The payment is lowest in the first year and rises by a percentage every year for the next five years. After this time, the payment remains the same for the life of the loan.

In the beginning of the loan term, the payments are not enough to cover the interest owed each month. This results in negative amortization, as with interest-only loans. This money is added to the balance of the loan. The higher payment in the fifth year of the loan and the years after the payment stabilizes will gradually bring down the additional principal balance which resulted from the low initial monthly payments.

The benefit of this type of a loan over an adjustable-rate mortgage is the predictability of the increase in payments. The borrower knows in advance how much the payment will increase in advance. With an ARM, the payment increase is unknown, since it is impossible to predict interest rate increases years ahead of time. Since the payment on a graduated payment mortgage increases at a fixed percentage, the payments are more predictable and tend not to get as high as some ARMs.

This type of loan is most often used for borrowers who are unable to qualify for a fixed-rate mortgage. These borrowers are in a situation where they need a lower payment for a few years but can handle a gradual increase each year. It is important to be sure the borrower will be able to handle the increase in the monthly payment. Borrowers anticipating a larger income over the next few years may do well with graduated payments.

FHA and VA Loan Programs

The Federal Housing Administration (FHA) insures mortgage loans. The FHA is part of the United States Department of Housing and Urban Development (HUD) and was founded by Congress during the Great Depression. The purpose was to make it easier for people to buy homes. The loan is insured by the FHA, which protects the lender.

FHA mortgages are available in either fixed or one-year adjustable-rate mortgages. In either case, the interest rate is often lower than for other types of loans. This is true for both fixed-rate and adjustable-rate mortgages. Another benefit of FHA loans is the lower down payment requirement. The down payment can be as low as 5 or even 3 percent. This is great for borrowers who do not have enough of a down payment for a conventional mortgage.

Qualifying for an FHA loan is easier than a conventional mortgage. The borrower's credit can be less than perfect. Major issues such as a recent bankruptcy, foreclosure, or default on a federal student loan can prevent the borrower from qualifying. However, typical credit blemishes or lower credit scores are not always a problem. FHA loans are often a good choice for first-time homebuyers, who often have a problem with little or no credit.

Requirements for an FHA mortgage:

- The borrower needs to show two years of continuous employment. This does not always have to be in the same job, but the same industry is preferred.
- The payments can be no more than 30 percent of the borrower's income.
- Two years must have passed since bankruptcy or three years after a foreclosure.
- The borrower must not be in default on a federal student loan.
- A borrower can have only one FHA mortgage at a time.
- There is a maximum loan amount which varies according to the area.
- The borrower must pay for private mortgage insurance.

VA (Department of Veterans Affairs) mortgages are available to veterans of the United States military. The VA loan program has been around since 1944, when it was included as part of the first GI Bill. The purpose of this program is to help our active military and former service men and women purchase homes. The money from the loan can be used to purchase a home, build a home, refinance, or make improvements.

The Department of Veterans Affairs is not the lender in these mortgages. The loans are insured by the VA, but underwritten by a private lender. Qualifying for these loans is easier than for other types of mortgages. As with FHA loans, there is a maximum loan amount for VA loans.

Eligibility for a VA loan:

- The borrower must have served 90 days of active duty during war time or 181 days during peace time.
- No dishonorable discharge from the military.
- National Guard members and members of the Reserves are eligible for VA loans after six years of service.
- The borrower cannot have a debt-to-income ratio greater than 41 percent.

The application process is similar to any other mortgage. The lender will pull a credit report and request information on income and any assets. In most cases, the loan can go to closing without further approval from the VA. The borrower is charged a funding fee by the VA. The fee can range from 1.25 to 2.15, depending on whether the borrower puts a down payment on the property.

A VA appraisal will be done of the property the borrower intends to purchase. The appraisal is required to determine the property value. The certificate of reasonable value is completed by the appraiser and used to determine the value of the home. This is done early in the process, since the loan cannot be for more than the amount of money listed on the certificate of reasonable value.

One of the biggest benefits of VA loans is the low down payment amounts. In some cases, loans can be found with no down payment requirement. In addition, for many loans, there are no closing costs. This saves a lot of money for the borrower.

The borrower must complete a Certificate of Eligibility to qualify for a VA loan. This is used by the VA to determine eligibility for the program. The borrower needs to complete a Request for a Certificate of Eligibility for VA Home Loan Benefits, VA Form 26-1880. This form and instructions can be found online at the VA Web site **www.homeloans.va.gov/elig1.htm**.

No-Document Loans

In some cases, the borrower may be unable or unwilling to show steady income. No-doc mortgages are often used for self-employed borrowers who do not receive a steady paycheck, but make enough money to afford the home. There is no income verification and the approval process is easier and faster. With no income or documentation to verify, approval is a straightforward process.

No-doc loans are not offered by many lenders. The lenders that offer these programs have strict guidelines. One is the borrower must have excellent credit to qualify. In addition, most lenders will require a larger down payment than would be required for a conventional mortgage. The reason for these requirements is the added risk to the lender with no documentation. The borrower pays a price for the convenience and privacy of a no-doc loan.

The biggest problem with no-doc loans is the higher cost. The higher down payment and higher interest rate can add significantly to the cost of the loan. The interest rate is higher with a no-doc loan than on a similar loan with all supporting documentation. Over time, this additional cost can add up. If rates drop, the borrower may want to consider refinancing the loan at some point to save money in interest payments.

As a mortgage broker, you will need to educate your clients on the advantages and disadvantages of no-doc loans. When you are talking with clients, you may be able to come up with a way to document the income and avoid the high cost of no-doc loans. If this is not possible, or the client does not want to disclose their income or financial information, a no-doc loan may be the best way to go.

Helping Customers Choose the Right Loan

Your job as a mortgage broker is to present your clients with a few different loan options. You should not show them every loan program that you have. The choices would be overwhelming. Instead, choose the best three to five loan programs to present to the client. You will need to explain the terms and conditions of each to help them understand the differences and make the right decisions.

The borrower's unique circumstances will play a large role in the decision. This is another reason to talk to your clients and get to know both their financial situation and future plans. These factors will weigh heavily in the decision on the best mortgage product. Talk about both their current situation and financial future, which will give you a better look at the big picture.

Adjustable rate mortgages are good for a lower initial interest rate. This is good for borrowers who have limited funds at the present time, but anticipate a substantial salary increase in the near future. These borrowers will not keep this loan forever. Most will use the low teaser rate to enjoy lower payments and then refinance in a few years to avoid the increase in rate.

If your clients are interested in taking this route, pay close attention to the prepayment policy of the lender for this loan. Make sure they will not have to pay a penalty to get out of the loan. The prepayment penalty period should not be longer than the initial teaser rate for a borrower looking to get out of the loan and avoid a large increase in payment. They will want to be able to refinance without a penalty for the loan to work for them.

If a borrower has good credit and can afford the payment and does not want to refinance in the future, a fixed-rate loan may be the best choice. The client will need to choose between a 15- and 30-year term for a fixed-rate home mortgage. The income and expenses of the borrower will help them make a decision. You will need to point out the differences in a few different fixed-rate loans to help them find the best deal.

The time you spend helping clients understand mortgages and the process is time well spent. Your clients will be happier with the level of service they have received. This will make them much more likely to refer friends, family, and coworkers to you in the future. You are making connections and building a list of leads and referrals with each client. Make the most of this time to connect with people and gain trust and respect.

Points and Closing Costs

The down payment is only part of the cost to the borrower when purchasing a home. Additional money will be needed for a variety of fees and charges. At settlement, two of the biggest chunks may be the points and closing costs. Borrowers have a lot of questions about these costs. Spend some time discussing the costs involved to help borrowers make sound financial decisions that are in their best interests.

Points

For many borrowers, the concept of paying points is one of the most confusing parts of taking a home mortgage. You need to be able to describe the purpose of points and determine the benefits and drawbacks of paying points for each client. Mortgage calculators are available on the Internet to determine the savings for mortgage points. An easy one to use is available at **www.dinkytown.net/java/MortgagePoints.html**. You can also purchase these calculators and others to use on your Web site. This is a great feature for clients and potential clients.

Points are fees charged by the lender in return for a lower interest rate. It can also be described as buying a discount on the interest rate. The number of points varies, depending on the loan and the desired interest rate. One point is 1 percent of the loan amount. On a $200,000 loan, each point costs $2,000. The more points the borrower pays, the lower the interest rate on the mortgage.

Say a borrower is taking a 30-year fixed rate loan for $200,000. With no points, the interest rate is 6.5 percent. With two points, the interest rate is 6 percent. How much money the borrower will save depends, in part, on how long they live in the house. Say the borrower lives in the house for ten years. He will save $3,560 in interest payments in that time. If he stays in the same house for only five years, having points will cost him $246 over that time period. The longer he stays in the house, the longer he will benefit from the lower interest rate and the more money he will save.

It would take this theoretical borrower a little over five years to break even after paying two points at closing. If the borrower plans to live in the house for a long period of time and raise a family in that home, paying the points at closing will definitely save money. However, if he only plans to live in it for three or four years, paying the points is not a good investment. The borrower's future plans should play a role in making decisions regarding points versus a higher interest rate.

Another factor is the amount of cash the borrower has for closing costs. If the borrower cannot afford the additional money that would be required at closing, the no-points option may be the better choice. In some cases, the points may be able to be financed. This depends on the lender and the loan.

The borrower can also deduct the points on his income tax for a first mortgage on his primary residence. If the loan is a refinance, the borrower can still deduct the points, but not in full. For a refinance, the points are deducted over the life of the loan, rather than all in the first year. This is calculated by dividing the points by the number of payments over the term of the loan. If the home is sold or refinanced again, the portion of the points that were not deducted would be deducted in that year.

Closing Costs

A variety of closing costs and fees are charged for mortgages. An estimate of these fees will be included in the Good Faith Estimate from the lender. As a mortgage broker, you need to be able to explain these fees to your client. An explanation of some of the common fees charged follows. Not all these fees will be charged with every loan, but it is important to understand all of them to be successful as a mortgage broker.

Appraisal Fee: This is included on nearly all mortgages. The appraiser will inspect the property and use homes that have been recently sold in the same area to determine the property value.

City Transfer Tax: This tax is charged whenever a property changes ownership.

County Property Taxes: This is the property tax that is paid yearly by property owners. For loans with an escrow account, part of this yearly tax may be collected at closing. These funds are then deposited in an escrow account.

Courier Fee: The costs incurred for delivering documents related to the mortgage loan.

Document Preparation Fee: This fee is sometimes charged by the title company for preparing the documents needed for closing.

Flood Insurance: If the property being mortgaged is located in a flood area, the borrower will be required to have flood insurance. Part or all of this premium will be collected at closing, depending on whether the borrower is planning to use an escrow account to pay taxes and insurance.

Homeowner's Insurance: This is required to protect both the borrower and the lender in the event something would happen to the property. If the borrower is using an escrow account to pay insurance, a few months may be collected in advance and deposited into the escrow account. If there is no escrow, the borrower may be required to pay the entire premium for the first year in advance.

Interest for the First Month: The lender will charge the interest from the day of closing until the first day of the month. For example, if the loan closes on the 15th, the interest will be charged from that date until the first day of the next month.

Inspection Fee: After the appraisal, the lender will have the property inspected. For new construction, the lender is making sure the house is completely finished. For existing homes, certain loan programs require additional expenses, such as FHA loans.

Loan Origination Fee: This is a fee charged by the lender for making the loan to the borrower.

Mortgage Broker's Fee: This is the fee charged by the broker. It will appear on both the Good Faith Estimate from the broker and the lender. This fee is a percentage of the total amount of the loan. The typical fee is between 1 and 2 percent of the total mortgage amount, depending on the loan and the difficulty in acquiring the loan.

Private Mortgage Insurance (PMI): This is insurance that the borrower may be required to carry. It is most common with a low down payment, usually less than 20 percent down.

Processing Fee: This fee is charged for processing the loan paperwork and documents.

Property Survey: The lender may require a survey of the property prior to closing.

Recording Fee: This is paid to the county for recording the deed or mortgage.

Settlement Fee: This fee is paid to the title company. The fee is charged for handling the financial transactions and transfers involved with closing.

Termite Inspection: Some lenders will require a termite inspection of the property prior to closing. This is often done in areas where termites are a problem.

Title Insurance: This is a guarantee that there are no liens on the property to be mortgaged. This protects both the borrower and the lender against any potential liens or claims against the property and former owners of that property.

Underwriting Fee: This fee is charged by the lender for reviewing the borrower's application.

Wire Transfer Fee: Funds are wired as part of mortgage transactions. There are small fees charged for this service.

Second Mortgages and Home Equity Lines of Credit

As a mortgage broker, you will be contacted for help in securing second mortgages or home equity lines of credit as well as primary mortgages and refinances. Some states require an additional license for mortgage brokers to broker second mortgages. Check with your specific state to determine if you need a separate license for home equity loans.

There is a wide range of loan products for homeowners who are looking to use the equity in their home. This is often done for home improvements, education, or debt consolidation. While terms, interest rates, and other factors may vary, there are two basic types of loans: second mortgages and home equity line of credit.

Second Mortgage

A second mortgage is a loan taken on the equity in a home. Taking a traditional second mortgage is a lot like taking a first mortgage. An appraisal will be done to determine how much equity is available to the homeowner. The borrower generally wants the money for a specific purpose, for example, to put in a pool or add a room onto the house.

The loan process is similar to a primary mortgage. The borrower takes a loan for a specific amount of money. The loan has a set term, for example, 5, 10 or 15 years. In most cases, the interest is deductible as it is with a primary mortgage. As long as the borrower can deduct interest on the primary mortgage on the property, he can deduct the interest on the second as well.

The documents required are also similar to a first mortgage. The lender will want to verify the borrower's income and credit report. An appraisal and title search will be required prior to closing on the second mortgage. The lender wants to be sure that he is just behind the primary mortgage as a lien holder on the property and that there are no other liens on the property.

Home Equity Lines of Credit

A home equity line of credit is money borrowed using the equity in the home as collateral. There are some significant differences between these loans and second mortgages. A home equity line of credit is a revolving line or credit, rather than a set amount of money, as in a second mortgage.

The borrower is approved for a specific amount of money, but the money is not taken in one lump sum, as with a standard second mortgage or home equity loan. The money is taken in draws. There is a set amount on most loans for the initial draw. This money is paid to the borrower after closing. With some loans, there is a minimum amount for each draw.

An appraisal will be done to determine the equity in the property. The amount of the total line of credit will depend on the loan-to-value ratio. This is the amount financed compared to the total value of the home. The lower the loan-to-value ratio, the more money will be available for the line of credit.

The terms vary from loan to loan. There are some things that the broker should compare when dealing with home equity line of credit loans. The repayment terms are one big difference in some line of credit loans. In some cases, the minimum monthly payment is not enough to pay off the loan at the end of the term. In this case, a balloon payment is due at that time.

Some lines of credit are interest-only loans. In this case, none of the payment is going toward the principal. As a result, the full amount of the principal would be due at the end of the term in a large balloon payment. The loan would have to be refinanced or a traditional second mortgage taken to pay off the loan balance. The borrower could also make additional principal payments each month to pay off the loan in time without a balloon payment.

The interest on a home equity line of credit is adjustable. It will fluctuate, so the monthly payment will change as interest rates go up and down. The interest on these loans works like other adjustable-rate mortgages. There are caps on how much the interest rate can change from one period to the next. Indexes are used to determine rates, as with ARMs.

CHAPTER

12

Commerical Market

When business owners require financing for commercial properties, they turn to commercial mortgage brokers. These professionals locate a lender with a loan program that will best suit the needs of the client, just as a broker would do for a borrower seeking a residential mortgage. As in residential loans, the broker will search for programs from several lenders to find the program that is the best fit for each client.

The commercial mortgage market can be lucrative for a skilled broker. Experience as a residential broker is not enough to succeed as a commercial broker. There are some significant differences between residential and commercial loans.

Mortgage brokers who work with homeowners often receive at least part of their training from their employers. This scenario does not work as well for commercial brokers. The training offered by most employers is not sufficient for success in this field. You will need to take courses and find training to prepare yourself for the commercial market. The National Association of Mortgage Brokers and other organizations offer training courses for the commercial market.

Check with your state regarding the type of licensing or certification that is required for commercial mortgage brokers. In some states, one license is used for both residential and commercial lending. However, some states require an additional certification for a broker to deal with commercial loans.

How Commercial Loans Are Similar to Private Mortgages

The concept of a commercial loan is similar to a residential mortgage. The borrower is requesting money from a lender to secure a property. This money is repaid in minimum monthly payments to the lender. The lender has a stake in the property. In the event the borrower fails to repay the money, the lender has the right to foreclose on the property. While the basic concept is the same, there are significant differences in these loans.

Differences Between Commercial and Residential Loans

There are significant differences between commercial and residential loans. One is the amortization of the loan. The typical home loan is for 15 or 30 years. The schedule is set up so that the loan will be paid off at the end of the term with regular monthly payments. This is not true with a commercial loan. These loans are often not fully amortizing. This means there will become due a balloon payment, generally in 10 years but this can vary.

With a residential mortgage, once the loan is approved, nothing needs to be supplied to the lender other than regular payments. In most commercial loans, there are ongoing requirements for reporting to the lender. This may be annual financial reports or cash flow information. These documents may need to be prepared by a certified public accountant.

Another difference is the ability to take a second mortgage or subsequent loan on the property. This may not be possible with some commercial lenders, even if there is sufficient equity in the building. The reason for this is the lender wants to remain the only entity with a claim to the property. If the borrower defaults on a second mortgage, the primary lender must join in the foreclosure to avoid losing out. Some companies will allow it, but only with written approval.

One of the first things you will need to determine is whether the client will be occupying the building for business purposes or using the property for investment. This is important because there is a big difference in underwriting the loan based on the use of the property.

Leasing and Renting Properties

Rent is a big factor in the world of commercial loans. Owners rent or lease space in commercial buildings for offices, stores, industrial purposes, and many other commercial uses. The rent collected is what provides the funds to pay the loan. Information on the market and rent that will be charged will be required by the lender. If the borrower has tenants secured for at least some of the space, it is easier to get an approval.

Skills Needed for the Broker

The most successful commercial brokers have a vast wealth of knowledge about business. Many have a college degree in business or finance. This educational background provides the commercial broker with knowledge of business and economic indicators that are relevant to their clients.

A degree in business is a great asset, but it is not enough to ensure success as a commercial mortgage broker. The successful professional needs to stay current on trends in the business world and economic forecasts. You will need to read a variety of information in business publications and be able to analyze the information and discuss the issues intelligently with your clients.

The ability to analyze data is an important skill for success as a commercial mortgage broker. You will need to be completely computer literate and be able to read and analyze spreadsheets and other graphic organizers that contain business information and trends. You will need to have knowledge of using databases and the ability to research and find information relevant to the commercial market.

Income Potential in the Commercial Market

The market is smaller and more competitive for commercial mortgage brokers. One reason is that not all commercial loans are handled by a broker. A smaller percentage of commercial customers use a broker compared to residential clients. Many commercial loans, particularly for a larger commercial development, are handled directly with the lender. This leaves a smaller pool of potential borrowers for the broker.

However, some commercial mortgages are handled by brokers.

As more people use brokers and become aware of the benefits of using a professional to help find the best loan, this number is likely to increase. Even with fewer clients, the loan amounts are much higher than with a home mortgage. This results in a higher income potential for the skilled commercial mortgage broker.

As in residential mortgages, the income potential of the broker is unlimited. The more loans that close, the more money the broker will make. The average income for commercial brokers depends on several factors. For a new broker, an income of up to $70,000 is not uncommon. With over three years of experience, the broker can easily make a six-figure salary.

The size of the projects and amount of the loan will influence the broker's income. The larger the amount of money being borrowed, the higher the commission for the broker. The number of loans closed is another factor that affects the income of the commercial broker. Since all brokers are paid at closing, the more loans that go to closing, the more money the broker will earn.

Achieving Success in the Commercial Market

The basic components to success in the commercial market are similar to that of the residential mortgage broker. You will need to build a database of potential clients and get people to refer business owners to you for their commercial lending needs. All mortgage brokers spend a significant amount of time finding new clients and cultivating business leads.

Referrals are a big part of finding new clients. Professionals who deal with business owners, such as lawyers and tax accountants, are a good source of quality referrals.

Common Mistakes Made by New Commercial Brokers

Working as a commercial mortgage broker can be a lucrative career with high income potential. However, there are some common mistakes that are made by new commercial brokers. Some of these mistakes can be quite costly and really cut into your income.

Not prescreening clients: During your initial conversation with any potential client, you should be prescreening the borrower. Taking the time to screen your potential clients will save you wasted time. In some cases, the person is only shopping around and has not decided to take a loan or use a broker. You do not want to invest too much of your valuable time on people who are not serious about taking a commercial loan or using your services.

Another important reason to prescreen you clients is to determine if the loan they are interested in securing is possible. Find out the details of the project and if the client or business has the capital to be approved for the loan. If they do not, you will be wasting your time putting together a loan application package that will ultimately be denied. Crunch some numbers in that first meeting or phone conversation to determine if the client is a good risk who is likely to win approval for the loan. A good software program can help you get the job done.

Failing to get a signed agreement: The days of the handshake deal are over. You must get a signed agreement with every client. This is imperative to protect yourself from loss. You will be investing a considerable amount of time to secure a commercial loan and you want to be paid for this time. Failing to get a signed agreement can cost you a lot of money and hurt your business.

This actually protects both the client as well as the mortgage broker. The client has an agreement that states the fees upfront so he knows exactly what your service will cost. The client will not have to worry about any surprises at closing. In addition, he will have the reassurance of not being surprised with unexpected fees.

Mistakes related to lenders: There are several mistakes that new commercial mortgage brokers make when dealing with lenders. One of these mistakes is using too many lenders. It is better to deal with fewer lenders than to try to deal with 50 or 100 lenders. Using a smaller number of lenders is a better way for the broker to build relationships and get to know commercial mortgage professionals. The effort you put forth to build these relationships will pay off in future loan situations.

Another problem with using a large number of commercial lenders is a failure to know and understand the programs each lender offers. When you have a smaller pool of lenders, it is easier to keep up with changes in programs and new programs being offered by each lender. Take the time to read the information sent to you and understand the requirements of each program; this will make the loan application process much smoother. Keeping updated on programs from 10 or 20 lenders is much easier than attempting to keep up with 100 lenders.

The commercial market is comprised of many different niche

markets, all under the umbrella of commercial real estate. The loan programs that are offered by lenders are targeted to specific real estate projects. For example, a loan for the construction of a new hotel is different from a loan to purchase a warehouse or office space. If you try to work on all types of commercial loans, it can get confusing. It will take time to learn the programs for each type of commercial property. In the beginning, it is best to concentrate on one or two types of projects so you can learn them well, rather than trying to learn 20 different commercial markets and loan types all at once.

CHAPTER 13

Expenses of Doing Business

Most mortgage brokers begin their careers working for a company. At some point in their careers, some of these brokers will decide to go out on their own and open their own company. Maybe this is your long-term goal. There are a lot of factors and expenses to consider when opening a business. Good planning is an important tool for success as a broker and business owner.

The initial cost of setting up a business depends on several factors. One is the overall size of the business. Will you be employing other brokers? Is the business a one-man show out of an empty room in your home? Obviously, the start-up costs for a firm that employs a few brokers in a downtown office will be much higher than working out of your home with one or even no other employees. The first step in starting your business should be to determine what the business will look like.

Another option is to purchase an existing brokerage firm. This can be a good opportunity, particularly if the firm has a good reputation and is a strong business. There are several benefits to buying an existing business including lower start-up costs. It takes considerable time, money, and energy to build a solid reputation and establish good relationships with clients and lenders. Purchasing an established firm allows you to utilize the contacts of that business while establishing your own reputation as the owner.

There are some important factors to consider when purchasing an existing company. If you were a broker in the firm, you may have a good picture of the financial health of the company and reputation in the community. Otherwise you will need to do some serious investigation before making an offer.

Ask for disclosure of all accounting information. These documents will provide valuable information about the business. You can request a financial audit done by a certified public accountant. This is a requirement in many states. If your state requires audited financial statements, the company should be able to provide you with copies of the statements from the last several years. This will give you a great picture of the company's financial situation over time.

Financing Start-Up Costs

Whether you are starting a one-man office or a larger company, you will need to have money for the initial costs. The amount of money needed will vary according to the size of the business, but funds will be needed regardless of the size. It will take a few months for you to bring in a steady cash flow. Money comes in when loans are closed, so cash is needed to pay for rent and other expenses while you are setting up loans for closing.

If you are planning to be self-employed out of your home, the start-up costs may be minimal. You may be able to fund it through your savings or using other personal funds or loans. If the business will be larger or you have no equipment to get started, a loan may be needed.

The Small Business Administration has a program to help small businesses get started. The 7a Loan Guaranty Program is the most basic of all loan programs. It is also the one that is most used by small business owners. This program is not a government loan. The SBA guarantees the loan, but a lender is the entity that loans the money to the business owner.

The lender has to participate in the program to qualify for the guaranty program. The majority of banks in the United States participate in the 7a program. The 7a Loan Guaranty Program protects the lender from loss. In the event a business owner defaults on the loan, the lender will be reimbursed for a percentage of the loan. The risk is shared between the lender and the SBA.

There are a few criteria that must be met for a business owner to qualify for the 7a Loan Guaranty Program. The factors for eligibility include the size of the business, the type of the business, how the loan proceeds will be used, and the availability of funds from other sources to cover the costs of business. The business owner applies with the lender, who then decides if a guaranty is required.

The character and financial history of the borrower is considered in approving loans under this program. All owners with a 20 percent or greater share in the business are required to personally guarantee the loan. The lender will look at the history of the borrowers to determine their history in terms of paying bills. Does the borrower have a good bill paying history? If so, it is seen as a good indication that he will repay this loan.

The maximum amount that can be borrowed through the 7a Loan Guaranty Program is two million dollars. This is more than enough to cover the needs of a mortgage broker. The amount that your business can get is determined by several factors. One of the biggest factors is the ability of the borrower to repay the loan. The cash flow of the business and potential income are taken into consideration in determining this factor.

The interest rate on these loans can vary by lender. You will need to shop the loan to a few lenders, just as you would for a client seeking a loan for a home. There are maximum interest rates that are set by the Small Business Administration. The maximum interest that can be charged is 2.25 percent above the prime rate for loans that mature in less than seven years. If the loan matures in seven years or more, the maximum interest rate that can be charged is 2.75 percent above the prime rate.

There are prepayment penalties with many of these loans. The penalty applies to loans with a maturity of 15 years or more and if the borrower is voluntarily paying the loan balance early. The prepayment amount must be more than 25 percent of the loan balance and the prepayment made in less than three years after the first money was received on the loan.

The percentage of this penalty varies, depending on which year the loan is paid off. The longer you keep the loan, the smaller the penalty when it is paid in full. During the first year of the loan, the prepayment penalty is 5 percent of the amount of the total balance that is being paid. During the second year, the prepayment penalty is 3 percent of the total balance. During the third year, the prepayment penalty drops to 1 percent. Because the total amount owed drops each year as well as the percentage, the longer you keep the loan the less you will have to pay in a penalty.

Office Expenses

The amount of money needed to fund initial and ongoing office expenses will vary widely, depending on the size of the business. There are some basic costs and fees associated with running a business, regardless of the size. To determine how much money you will need to borrow, you need to determine the start-up costs of your business and the amount of cash you need in reserve while you are building the business.

Office Space Options

One of the biggest decisions you will make early on is where your office will be located. This is the place where you will be conducting your business and sometimes meeting with clients. You have a few choices for the location of your office space. You could rent an office, buy office space, or create an office in a room in your home. There are several factors to consider when making this decision.

The first is location. While the bulk of your work will be done over the phone, there are times when you will need to meet with clients face to face. For this, you will need a convenient location for your office. Is your home suitable for this? If you have a home that is centrally located and easy to find, this will not be a problem. If you live in a rural area or other out-of-the-way place, you may want an office that is closer to the center of town or at least in a more populated area.

If you have decided that you want a space that is not in your home, you still have choices to make. You can either rent or purchase office space. Most mortgage brokers lease, rather than buy office space. There are benefits and drawbacks to each choice. You need to weigh your options and consider your future plans to make the best decision for your business.

Benefits of leasing office space:

- Renting space in a desirable area is often less expensive than purchasing similar property.
- Less money spent results in more cash available for other aspects of your business.
- In many areas, there is greater availability for leasing an office space.
- There are none of the usual headaches associated with property ownership, such as paying for improvements or repairs.

Benefits of owning your office:

- The monthly cost will remain the same from year to year if you have a fixed-rate loan. Rent increases and you end up paying a higher amount each month after a few years in the same location.
- You are building equity. Owning property is an investment, whether it is an office or a home. As your property value increases, you build equity in the building.

- If the building is larger than you need, you can always rent out some of the space to another business. This results in additional income for you. The rent you collect can be put toward the monthly mortgage payment.

- There are tax benefits to owning your own property. You can deduct mortgage interest and property taxes, as you do with a home mortgage.

- The space can be sold when you are ready to retire, giving you additional savings for retirement.

Home Offices: Zoning, Permits, and Licensing

Most mortgage brokers start out by opening a small office at home. There are a few benefits to having your office at home. When you get up in the morning, you are already at work. The cost associated with commuting between the home and office is saved when you do not have to travel to work. There is a time savings as well. Assuming a 30-minute commute each way, you will save five hours in travel time each week. This time can be spent focusing on your business.

Having an office in your home is much less expensive than leasing office space. You are saving other costs as well, such as utilities and insurance. Since you can deduct a portion of your home expenses, such as mortgage interest, insurance, and utility costs, there are tax advantages in addition to saving money. The home office seems like the perfect solution for the broker looking to open a one-man office.

Working from home is not always as easy as it seems, as it is easy to get distracted when your office is in your home. To be successful in a home-based business, you must be good at organizing your time and structure your work day. Are you the type of person who can focus on work and not be easily distracted by family, the phone, and household projects? These factors have a way of creeping in and eating up a lot of your work day. If you are not good at shutting out these distractions, an alternate location for the office may be your best choice.

Motivation can be another problem when you are working from home. To be successful in a home office, you must have the ability to stay motivated and continue working toward your goals. A good business plan can help with motivation and keeping you on track. Breaking down tasks into daily jobs is important for structuring your time.

Before opening a home office, check with your local zoning board. In some areas, it is against zoning regulations to operate a business out of your home. In other areas, a variance or conditional use can be given to accommodate the business. Take the time to check the laws in your area. You do not want to be surprised with a fine and possibly closed down for failing to abide by the laws in your area.

People who attempt to circumvent the zoning process are often turned in by their neighbors. Sometimes neighbors get annoyed by the number of people coming in and out of the house or parking on the street. This is unlikely to be a problem with a mortgage broker. It is doubtful that you will have a steady stream of cars pulling in and out of the driveway.

In other cases, the neighbor may have a grudge against the business owner. In retaliation for some perceived wrongdoing, the disgruntled neighbor calls the local governmental body or zoning officer and turns in the business. Without the proper zoning approval or permits, it is possible that you would have to close the doors on your business. To avoid these problems, follow the proper procedure.

You may also want to talk to your closest neighbors. Tell them what you are planning to do. You are not asking their permission, which is actually up to the local ordinances. Communicating with them is still a nice thing to do and will help prevent any problems later. You never know what will come of the conversation. You may walk away with a referral or two.

Depending on where you live, you will need a business license or permit. This is not your mortgage broker's license. It is a license to do business that is granted by either the city or county. Your local zoning officer can help you determine what you need in your town. If you are planning to put out a sign, ask about the local ordinances regarding signage and how you can apply for a permit, if needed.

Equipment Expenses

All business owners need to make an initial investment in office equipment. This can be done with funds from loans or your savings. Another option for equipping a home office is to lease the equipment you need. Leasing is a good option if you do not want to use a good portion of your available credit for purchasing equipment.

You will need a computer with Internet access. It can be either a desktop or a laptop model. The benefit of a laptop is that you can take it with you when you are out of the office. Invest in a quality computer with decent speed and memory to meet the needs of the software you will be using. High-speed Internet access is faster, which will help you work more efficiently.

Once you have purchased your computer, you will need software. The first thing you should buy is a comprehensive antivirus software and firewall to protect your investment from the not-so-nice people on the Internet. Once the software has been installed, be sure to update the virus definitions on a regular basis. New viruses and worms are being created all the time. Some programs have an automatic update and will look for updated information regularly or prompt you to do so.

There is some other basic software that you will need for your business. Most computers come with a Windows operating system, such as Windows XP. You will need software for word processing, creating spreadsheets, and maintaining a database of clients and referrals. Microsoft Office contains applications to meet all these needs.

You will also need software that is specific to the mortgage industry. One of the most popular programs is Calyx Point. According to the company, 68 percent of all mortgage brokers use Calyx Point. The software comes with all forms and reports needed for every stage in the process, including loan marketing, prequalification, and origination. The company offers training classes and technical support. You can enjoy a free live demo of this software at **www.calyxsoftware.com/order/demo.asp**.

There is a wide range of other software that is marketed to mortgage brokers. How much or how little of this you purchase is completely your call. Your budget will determine how much you can afford as well, since some of these programs can be quite pricey. Software is available to generate leads, calculate payments, calculate the terms and interest of loans, and much more. You can always get a few basic features and add more software as you earn money or after you acquire a loan.

You will need a printer for printing forms and reports. Sometimes a cheap printer will come bundled with a computer. That is a nice gesture, but will not serve your purposes. You will also need a fax machine and a copier. An all-in-one printer, scanner, fax, and copy machine is the least expensive way to get all the functions you will need in your home office. The price is far less than it would be if you purchased separate machines.

Once you have bought all this great office equipment, you will need to find a location for it all. The first thing you will need is a computer desk and chair. If you are using a laptop, a regular desk will do. Make sure your desk is large enough to provide room for your computer and a work space for you. Invest in a comfortable chair that offers support for your back. You will be spending a significant amount of time sitting in that chair.

When planning your home office, consider how you will organize your equipment and supplies. File cabinets, shelving, and cabinets to hold equipment and office supplies will keep your office clean and give it a more professional look. Consider the size and layout of the room when selecting cabinets and before hanging shelves. A good plan will help you maximize the space and create a comfortable work environment.

Estimated Equipment Costs	
Equipment	**Average Cost**
Office furniture (desk, chair, file cabinet)	$400 to $800
Computer and printer	$2,000
Software, Internet connection	$500 to $1,500
Telephone, answering machine, fax	$200 to $500
Office supplies	$300
Organizational supplies, shelves, cabinets	$300 to $500

Business Structure

When starting your own company, you will need to decide how to structure the business. There are four choices in most states for structuring your new business: sole proprietorship, partnership, corporation, and limited liability company (LLC). The best structure will depend on several factors, including the size of the business. Many brokers start out as either a sole proprietor or partnership. For more personal liability protection, the LLC is a viable alternative.

There are tax and liability implications for each type of business structure. It is best to consult with an accountant to determine which business structure would best meet your needs. In the first year or so, you will be building your business and your income may not be large. However, as your business grows the tax implications may be significant. An accountant can best discuss the alternatives and help steer you in the right direction.

Sole proprietorship is the simplest business structure. The only requirement is that the mortgage broker is engaging in business and offering services to clients. In this structure, you are the owner, manager, and employee of the business. The problem with this structure is that you have personal financial liability in the event the business was to fail. Creditors or the government can come after your personal assets if you default on loans or get behind in taxes.

Partnership is often used when two or more mortgage brokers open a firm together. Some brokers feel that by combining their resources with another broker, the business will be on stronger ground and there is a greater potential for success. The structure is similar to the sole proprietorship. A partnership agreement is created to spell out the responsibilities of each partner in the operation of the business. All partners have unlimited liability, just as the sole proprietor is liable if something goes wrong with the business.

The corporation is the most complicated business structure to set up or maintain. For legal and tax purposes, the corporation is a separate entity. The corporation is run by the board of directors and the officers. The corporation offers liability protection to the business owners. The process of structuring a corporation is the most involved of any business structure; you must file articles of incorporation. If you want to structure your business in this way, you will need an attorney and an accountant.

There are two basic types of corporations, the C corporation and S corporation. The main difference between the two involves taxes. The C corporation is a bit more complicated to set up and maintain. The IRS taxes C corporations at the corporate level and at the individual level. The corporation is taxed on the profits and shareholders are taxed on monies received by the corporation including salaries and commissions. This double taxation can be significant when the shareholders and company officers are also the employees.

The S corporation is not a separate entity for tax purposes. The money is distributed to the employees as profit and not as salary. The corporation does not pay taxes on profits or income. The employees of the business (the brokers) pay the taxes by filing individual tax returns. For most brokers that want to structure the business as a corporation, the S corporation is the best choice because it offers the liability protection without the double taxation.

The limited liability company is a fairly new business structure in many states. This structure offers the business owner liability protection as he would have with a corporation. The LLC can be set up in several ways to give the business owner tax benefits and reduce personal liability. To set up this structure, articles of organization must be filed with your state. A filing fee is collected at that time. This fee varies from state to state. The partners in an LLC file an operating agreement that states the rules for the operation of the business. Annual reports are not required with an LLC.

Cost of Marketing and Advertising

One of the largest expenses you will have throughout the life of your business is marketing and advertising. The best place to start is with an overall budget for a specific period of time. You can use a monthly or annual figure. Once you have determined how much you can afford to spend, you will need to decide how to spend that money for the best return on your investment.

Newspaper advertising is often used to find potential borrowers that live in a specific area. The cost of advertising in the newspaper can vary widely, according to the size of the publication and the circulation. This is the number of papers sold in a day. The cost of advertising in a larger paper can break the budget if you are not careful. Full-page ads in the largest papers in the country run well over $100,000. In a small city, the figure can be over $20,000, which is still not possible for most brokers. Small, local papers charge a fraction of these prices.

Smaller ads, such as a quarter page or smaller, may be in the budget. You will need to contact your local paper to determine the exact cost for the size of the ad you want. Deal directly with the newspaper, rather than an advertising firm. The cost will be less because you will not be paying the ad company's fee on top of the cost of the ad.

Radio ads are effective at targeting a specific market. The rates for advertising depend on the size of the station. The cost varies from a few hundred to a few thousand dollars, depending on the station and the time of day the ad is played. Larger stations with a larger audience charge more than smaller stations. The frequency, or number of times the ad is played, also affects the cost of advertising on the radio.

Meet with several different radio stations before making a decision regarding advertising. Compare the proposals from each station. Look for the frequency, information about their ability to reach your targeted audience, and the cost involved. It is tempting to go with the lowest cost, particularly for a new business with a limited advertising budget. This is not always the best road to take.

If the station does not reach your target market, the money you spend will be wasted. The best indication of the effectiveness of the message will be seen in how much of a response it generates.

Paying $500 for an ad that does not generate any business is a complete waste of money. It makes no difference that the cost was far lower than the competitor. An ad that costs $3,000, but brings in $5,000 in revenue is worth the money spent, even though it cost a lot more than the cheap ad.

You will need to hire a professional production company to create your radio ad. A company with extensive experience in creating radio advertising is the best choice. This is not a do-it-yourself job. A professional will know how to effectively format the ad to get the most attention for your business. An ad that is created by an amateur will sound amateur and will be less likely to bring the results you want.

Television ads can be very expensive. For this reason, many mortgage brokers do not even consider a television spot as part of their advertising. There are two costs to consider in advertising on television. The cost of air time is only part of the picture. You also need to consider the cost of producing the commercial. The cost of a commercial can range from $1,000 to over $300,000, depending on the length of the commercial and the company producing it. Smaller, local production companies may charge a much lower fee than larger companies.

The cost of air time varies according to the market. A national commercial will be hundreds of thousands of dollars for a 30-second spot. This is cost prohibitive for all but the largest companies in the country. Smaller and medium-sized television markets are not out of the question. Air time can be found at these stations for a few hundred to a few thousand dollars, depending on the station.

Direct Marketing

The cost of direct mailings depends on the material you want to have printed. Half-page or quarter-page mailings are less expensive than full-page ads. Will material be printed on one side or both sides of the page? This all adds to the cost of the mailing. The rates vary, but a good, complete package will generally cost between $300 and $700 per thousand copies. The other cost involved is postage. Some packages include postage, but others do not. You can buy bulk-rate postage through the post office.

Ordering postcards and other printed materials in bulk can save a lot of money. The cost per unit is often significantly lower with a larger quantity. The bulk of the expense involves the initial setup and layout of the postcard. The cost of printing a larger quantity is relatively low, since the initial setup fee will only be paid once.

If you do not offer a deal with a specified deadline, you can use the remaining postcards at a later date. You will still have the expense of postage, but you will not have to pay again for the printing of the materials. This solution is great for brochures and printed materials that contain information that does not change frequently. Order a larger quantity and put the extras in a filing cabinet for future use.

Compare the costs from a few different direct marketing companies before you make a decision. What is included in the cost? Comparing only the total cost can be like comparing apples and oranges. If one package includes a lot more than the other, the company that appears to be less expensive on the surface could end up costing a lot more.

Monitoring the Results

It is important to monitor the results of all advertising campaigns. Determine which methods of advertising are the most profitable and are bringing you the most business. You can do this by asking your clients and people who call for information where they heard about your business. Keep a record of each person and where he or she learned about your service.

If you are a little more organized, you can determine which avenue is bringing you the greatest number of loan closings. For example, one ad can bring you 100 phone calls, but only 5 clients. Another ad may only result in 50 phone calls, but 8 loan closings. If you are only keeping track of the number of calls, it can look like the ad that brought 100 phone calls was a more successful campaign. By digging a little deeper, you will find that the smaller ad resulted in more loan closings.

Monitoring the results of your ad campaigns will help you determine where to spend your advertising budget in the future. Advertising is an ongoing cost of doing business, but there is a limit to the budget. Choosing the most profitable advertising can help you get the most for your advertising dollar.

Insurance

Insurance is one area mortgage brokers tend to overlook early in their careers. There are various types of insurance that you should consider to cover you, your business, and any employees.

Liability Insurance: All brokers should have liability insurance, whether working from home with no employees or in a larger firm that employs several brokers. Liability insurance covers you and your employees in the event you are sued. This may seem improbable, but it can happen. If a loan does not close, you are at risk of having a suit filed by the client, lender, or both. Your insurance professional is the best source of information about a policy that will meet the needs of your business.

Property Insurance: Many mortgage brokers who work from home offices mistakenly assume their homeowner's insurance will cover the home office. This is often not the case. Expenses related to your home office and any equipment loss may not be covered by your homeowner's insurance. In some cases, additional coverage needs to be added to your existing policy to cover the office expenses. Speak to your insurance agent to determine what is needed to ensure your business investment is protected.

Business Income Insurance: You have liability insurance to protect you against lawsuits and property insurance to protect your business, but what about your income in the event of an incident that suspends the operation of your business? This is where business income insurance comes in handy. A business income policy will help cover the expenses while your business cannot be operated. Coverage varies, according to the policy, so check with your insurance professional to determine the policy that will offer the best protection for your company.

Health Insurance: Whether you are working alone or employing others, you need health insurance. If you are a self-employed individual, you still need coverage for you and your family. If you are employing people, this is an important benefit to offer your staff. It is easier to attract and retain good employees when they are offered benefits. Health insurance is a big expense, but it is not as difficult for the self-employed person to obtain a policy as it was several years ago.

You can speak to an insurance professional about options for health insurance. In addition, inquire about joining a group of other self-employed individuals. These groups have been formed to allow self-employed people to enjoy the lower rates offered to larger companies. The Internet can be a good source of information for comparing policies. Several Web sites offer this service; two of which are listed below.

Ehealthinsurance.com allows you to view and compare policies from several companies online. This site does not sell insurance, but you can get an idea of what is out there, in terms of both coverage and cost. The site offers detailed information for making a comparison between plans.

The site makes it easy to find the information you need. When searching, you click on the type of policy you are interested in obtaining. You will fill out a short form on the site stating your preferences, when you want the coverage to begin, your gender, and date of birth. Your ZIP code will need to be entered to help locate information on plans available in your location.

Another great feature of this site is the ability to view the plans in detail. You can even check to be sure your doctor and preferred hospital are affiliated with each policy. Once you have determined which plan you want, it is easy to apply online.

2insure4less.com is a referral service for consumers to find information on health care plans. It is not an insurance company and they do not sell insurance plans. You find and compare information about available insurance in your area and estimates for coverage. This is done by an automated process. Your information is then forwarded to three different agents who will supply you with detailed quotes to compare and select a plan.

This site has a search feature to compare plans. Enter your ZIP code to get started. You will enter the type of plan, your birth date, and answer a few short questions. Additional information will be asked about the number of dependants on the plan. This will help ensure a more accurate quote for a family plan. After you enter your information, a page will appear with a list of companies offering plans in your area. Click to compare the plans.

CHAPTER

14

Business Plan

A good place to start is with a plan for your business. There are several reasons to write a detailed business plan. If you will be applying for a small business loan, the lender will want to see a detailed plan. Think of your business plan as a proposal to the lender. The plan gives the lender a good picture of your business, future plans, and the viability of your business.

Even if you are not planning to take out a loan to start your business, you will want a business plan. Think of it as a blueprint to follow on your path to success as both a broker and business owner. Your business plan spells out your goals for your business. This can help keep you on track for meeting your goals and objectives. A well-thought-out business plan is an important tool for success.

A well-thought-out and detailed business plan can mean the difference between success and failure. A detailed plan that includes both short- and long-term goals gives vision and helps direct your business. It is easy to get caught up in the daily work involved in running a business; this can get in the way of forward momentum. Following a detailed plan is a great way to keep you on track to reaching your goals.

Components of a Business Plan

Each business plan will be unique, just as each business is unique. There are certain sections that are considered to be standard on a business plan. The lender will be looking for these sections to approve a loan. Make sure your plan includes an introduction, financial information, marketing plan, operational structure, and a conclusion where you sum up the overall plan and offer additional information.

The introduction is where you tell the lender about yourself and your business. This is where you are selling yourself to the lender. Things to include in the introduction:

- Description of your business and goals for the business. If you plan to focus on a particular market, such as self-employed borrowers, include this here.

- What is the legal structure of the business? Is it a sole proprietorship or a partnership?

- Include information about the need or demand for your business.

- How is your business different from that of your competitors?

- Why will your business succeed? Many new businesses fail. What is it about you and your plan that will result in success?

- Include information about yourself and your experience as a broker. Highlight any past success, for example if you have worked for a company and have brought in the highest amount in loans for the past two years.

The financial information section of your business plan is where you will include all the relevant financial information to show how you will fund the business. This gives the lender some insight into your ability to repay the money you are planning to borrow. In this section, you should include:

- A detailed budget showing the total costs involved in operating your business.
- All of your projected expenses, including rent, salaries, and all other operating expenses.
- The cash you have available to fund some of the business expenses. Include your own savings, funds from loans, money from partners or investors, and any other sources of money that you have available.
- Projections for the income of the business. Do not make wild predictions that are ten times your current annual salary. Keep the projections reasonable to gain the respect and trust of the lender.
- What is the break-even point for investments versus income?
- How will you deal with ongoing expenses and unexpected costs? Include a safety net for income projections versus actual costs. This is often expressed in a percentage.
- How will you pay your business and personal bills in the early months? Remember that it will take some time

to build a steady cash flow and close loans on a regular basis. You need to show that you can afford to live during that period of time.

The marketing plan is an important component of the overall business plan. This is a blueprint for how you will advertise your services. This section should contain information about the costs and type of advertising you will use to reach potential clients. Things to include in this section:

- Information on the demand for mortgage brokers in your area.
- Information on the current mortgage market in your area and forecasts for the future.
- What is your marketing strategy?
- Where do you plan to advertise?
- How will you use referrals to build your business?
- How large is your current client database?
- What is the estimated cost for all advertising planned?

In the business operations section you will go into more detail about the day-to-day operations of your business. Who will run the business and make decisions? If you are a sole proprietorship, the answer will probably be you. In businesses with a partner or larger companies with several employees, the answer may not be so simple.

If you have a partner, who will make the day-to-day decisions regarding the business? Will you make decisions together or will one of you act as an office manager and update the other as needed? This information will also be included in the partnership agreement, but a summary should also appear in the business plan. Things to consider:

- Who will manage the business?
- How will payroll be handled?
- Who will hire and fire employees?
- Who will make decisions regarding equipment and make the purchases?

The competition is one thing many business owners do not address in a business plan. Do not make this mistake. Lenders and investors know there is competition for every business. They like to see a business owner who is well aware of his competition and has a solid plan to set himself apart from the competition. Without information on the competition in the plan, it can look like the borrower is unprepared to compete in the marketplace with other businesses.

Be sure to include information on your competition and any other obstacles to success. Showing an awareness of potential pitfalls and a plan for how you will deal with them will impress the lender. You will be seen as a serious professional who has given careful consideration to all aspects of the business.

The conclusion is one section that is sometimes forgotten when people write business plans. Do not forget to include this in your plan, especially if you are planning to take a loan to help finance your business. The conclusion is where you summarize the information included in your business plan and add other relevant information that may not have fit elsewhere in the plan. Things to include in the conclusion:

- Short- and long-term goals for the business
- Objectives to be met to attain each of these goals.
- Financial goals for the early years of the business as well as longer-term financial projections
- A summary of your experience and plan to achieve success in your new business

Tips for Writing a Business Plan

The length of the business plan will depend on who the readers are. If the plan is going to be used as part of your loan application, you will want it to be succinct and professional, rather than too wordy. Include the relevant information, but leave out the long explanations of how you will reach every objective on the plan. The typical business plan for the lender is between 10 and 20 pages, depending on the size of the business.

If you are not planning to apply for a loan and are writing the plan for planning purposes, it can be as long as you want. There are benefits to including a lot of information in this type of plan. Spelling out what you plan to do in great detail and including a timeline for reaching your goals will help keep you on track. The size of a plan that will be used by the business owner can be anywhere from 50 pages or more.

Writing a business plan is not a one-time deal. The first plan you write is only your plan for starting your business and goals for getting it off the ground. Updating and changing your business plan should be a regular task. You do not need to work on your plan every day or even every week, but you do need to review it regularly.

Setting and Achieving Goals

Since you will be including short- and long-term goals, you should review your short-term goals and objectives on a regular basis. Are you meeting the goals on the schedule you had planned? If so, how can you continue to grow or reach the next set of objectives faster? If you are not reaching your goals as quickly as planned, what has gone wrong? What can you do to meet the objectives? You can update or change your objectives and schedule as needed.

When writing goals, keep in mind that all goals should be:

- **Specific:** Write your goals with plenty of detail. What exactly are you going to do? What steps are you going to take toward achieving that goal? It is better to include as much detail as possible in your goals.

- **Measurable:** How will you know you have reached your goal or are moving in the right direction? To be certain, the goals need to be measurable. This is not only for your long-term goals, but for each of your short-term goals. You are more likely to stick with your goals when you can measure your progress along the way.

- **Realistic:** A long-term goal such as, "I will control 80 percent of the mortgage market in my area within one year," is a measurable and specific goal, but this goal is not realistic; certainly not within a year and maybe not ever. Be sure the goals you are setting are reachable within a reasonable amount of time. When you have realistic goals that you are able to achieve, you will be more likely to succeed.

- **Challenging:** You want your goals to be realistic and achievable, but resist the temptation to make them too easy. Write goals that you will find challenging and enjoy tackling. The trick is to make it challenging, while keeping the goals realistic.

- **Fixed:** Goals should be set for a fixed period of time. This will help you stay focused on achieving a goal. The time period for achieving any goal should be long enough to take the steps necessary to reach the goal but short enough to keep you focused and challenged.

Some business owners write two plans: one for the lender and investors and the other for their own use. The second plan is more detailed and includes specific information regarding each goal and objective stated in the plan. These notes are for you and will help you stay on track to reach your goals. In a good plan, each objective for the goal is structured to help you reach the goal.

Specific strategies can be included for overcoming obstacles and meeting objectives. Since this plan is for your own planning purposes, it is up to you what to include or leave out. The more detailed the plan, the easier it will be for you to follow. It will also be easier to measure your success. You will be able to see exactly where you are meeting your objectives and what areas need improvement. This helps you focus your efforts and achieve success.

As you re-evaluate and rewrite your goals, perform an honest assessment of how things are going. Pretend it is someone else's business that you are evaluating. Make a list of the strengths and weaknesses you see in regard to meeting your goals and objectives. Look at each weakness individually and write a plan on how to improve that specific area. What steps can you take to overcome that weakness or improve performance in that area? Do the same thing with the strengths of your business. How can you use these strengths better to reach your goals?

CHAPTER

15

Using Technology

Today's mortgage broker has the benefit of technology to help grow and maintain a business. Technology gives brokers the freedom to work from anywhere. Software programs help brokers prepare loan application packages and communicate with lenders. The Internet offers abundant opportunities for generating leads and marketing the business.

Cell phones may not seem like cutting-edge technology, but a good cell phone is a necessary piece of equipment for every mortgage broker. You need to stay in contact with clients and lenders at all times.

There are a multitude of choices when shopping for a cell phone. Phones have a wide range of features and prices. The price rises with the number of features offered in the phone. Before you go shopping, decide which features are most important. This will make comparing phones easier.

There are a few basic things to consider when purchasing a cell phone. Choose a phone with a good-quality lithium battery with as much talk time as possible. Be sure to get a charger for in the house and one for the car. These can be plugged into a wall outlet or a cigarette lighter so you never have to worry about a dead battery. A hands-free device allows you to talk without holding the phone. This is convenient when you are speaking to a client while accessing information on your laptop.

A Bluetooth headset will allow you to talk hands free. Bluetooth technology offers a range of other benefits to a mortgage broker. It allows you to connect devices, such as laptops, phones, PDAs, and printers. You can exchange information from one device to the other, provided they are within range. This includes wireless capability for your PDA and laptop.

You want to ask about the address book in the phone. Get one with as much space as possible. This will allow you to program entries for clients, various lenders, and other professionals you work with. Cheaper phones may have less room for entries. This is one feature to compare.

Personal Digital Assistant (PDA)

A personal digital assistant (PDA) is a small, handheld computer. Newer models are a compact size that easily fits in a pocket. The screen is larger than the screen on a cell phone. A stylus or small keyboard can be used to enter information into the PDA.

There are many benefits to owning a PDA for the broker who frequently works out of the office. A PDA allows you to store phone numbers, e-mail addresses, and Web site information. You can also make calculations on your PDA, which is handy when you are speaking to a client and need a quick calculation. A digital calendar allows you to keep your schedule at your fingertips and access it from anywhere. You can even access the Internet with wireless capability.

Some higher-priced cell phones have features to replace a PDA. There are varying opinions on this among brokers. Some feel having one device is sufficient and less expensive. It is also one less piece of equipment to be carrying around with you. Others like having two devices. One reason for this is to have a backup of all your information in your PDA. If the phone is lost or the battery is dead, you can still access your information through the PDA.

The phones that replace a PDA are expensive. If you need to buy both, this may be a good investment. If you already own a PDA or a cell phone, the several-hundred-dollar price tag may feel like a bit too much. These phones are also quite a bit larger and bulkier than either a cell phone or a PDA.

Laptops are a great piece of equipment for mortgage brokers. Look for a laptop that is wireless compatible. This will allow you to access the Internet, check your e-mail and access information at meetings, in restaurants, airports, hotels and many other places. If you have a Bluetooth headset, you can use that to access the Internet as well.

When shopping for a laptop, get the best one you can afford. Most of the newer laptops are much slimmer and easier to carry than even a few years ago. This makes carrying it with you more convenient. Be sure to get a long-life battery and purchase at least one spare to extend the time it can be used without recharging. Using the plug when possible also saves the battery, but there are times when no plug is available.

Pay the additional money for the extended warranty. Repairs to a laptop are very expensive, so you want the peace of mind offered by the warranty. Consider the availability of tech support. Paying a bit less may not be a savings if you do not have tech support available when you need it. Look for technical support that you can access 24 hours per day, seven days per week.

You will want to install all the mortgage broker software that you have on your desktop computer on the laptop as well. You will want to be able to access this software when meeting with potential clients or when working away from the office. You can synchronize the laptop with your desktop computer to transfer and update information.

Software Programs

There are a variety of software programs available for mortgage brokers. The features of each program vary. Most software programs cost a couple of hundred dollars. This is money well spent and a good program will help in the loan application process and in running your business and tracking your loans.

Features of Mortgage Broker Software

Although the features available will vary depending on the software you choose, there are some good features to look for when choosing a program for your business. Become familiar with some of the available features to determine which ones you need for your business. Here are some things to consider when selecting a program-

Loan marketing is a big part of the mortgage broker's job. Finding leads for new loans is an ongoing concern and a good software program can help. You can use the software to print flyers with comparisons for a specific property. You just have to input different scenarios for interest rates and closing costs to generate the comparisons.

Prequalification for a mortgage is a good idea for prospective homeowners. When they are prequalified, shopping for a home is easier. The borrower will know how much to spend and the prequalification can help the borrower negotiate the price with the seller. Software can help with the prequalification process so you can tell borrowers how much they can get for a home loan.

Loan origination features in software programs save a lot of time in the application process. With a good program you can quickly complete the application, Good Faith Estimate, and Truth in Lending statements. These forms can then be electronically transmitted to lenders for approval.

Automated underwriting features in software programs make communicating with lenders easy. Look for a program that allows you to interface with Fannie Mae and Freddie Mac software to transfer information to underwriters easily. This makes getting an answer for your clients faster.

Loan processing features help with putting together a loan package to submit to lenders. The data that you enter on one screen is transferred to other screens without the need to re-enter the information over and over again. Since there are many forms that need to be completed for a loan package, this is a great feature to look for in a program.

Reporting tools are useful for keeping track of the loans you are working on and allow you to quickly find the status of a specific loan application. A good program will automatically tell you if any documents are missing from the loan package, or you can run a general check that will look for missing documents on all loan files. Reports can be generated for one loan or all the loans in your files.

Calyx Point is a popular software program that is used by residential mortgage brokers. The company advertises the fact that about 68 percent of all U.S. mortgage brokers use Calyx Point in their businesses. Other popular programs include Encompass, ezFinance, and Captaloans.

There are software programs that are made specifically for commercial brokers. One such program is Commercial Real Estate's Final Conclusion. This program provides the questions to ask your broker in an easy-to-follow format. There are questions for each type of commercial real estate project. The broker enters the required data and prints the relevant reports. The reports include a loan investment analysis, capitalization rates, analysis of income and expenses, maximum loan amount, sensitivity report, discounted cash flow, and a lease analysis with summary.

When selecting a software program, the best choice will depend on your business and the features you think will be most useful. Compare a few programs to select the one that will work best for you. Compare the features offered to find the most inclusive program for your budget. This information can be found on the Web site for the manufacturer of each program.

Some sites will allow you to download a free trial version of the software. This allows you to try out some of the features before you shell out your money. If you are having trouble making a decision, you can download a free trial for a few different programs and try them out. This will help you make the best choice for your business.

Other Useful Software for Mortgage Brokers

- Credit repair software to help borrowers with credit problems improve their credit scores to get a better deal on a home loan.

- Direct-mail management software to help create and manage your direct mail marketing campaigns.

- Lead-generating software to help with finding new prospects.

- Financial calculators such as mortgage qualification, payments, refinance calculations; debt consolidation and renting versus owning calculations make your job faster and much easier.

- Accounting software to track your business income and expenses. This is also useful when tax season approaches.

- Automatic backup is useful for preventing data loss. A built-in daily back up is a convenient way to protect all your information. There are many ways to back up your information. Choose the one that is best for your needs.

- Microsoft Office is not specifically for mortgage brokers, but offers many benefits for your business. This software is an office suite, created by Microsoft. There are three applications to Office: PowerPoint, Word, and Excel. The Pro version includes Access and Schedule Plus.

- PowerPoint allows you to create slide show presentations on your computer. You can include text, photographs, charts, graphs, and other information. This is useful when making presentations to clients or other professionals, such as Realtors.

- Word is a word processing program that is well known.

- Excel allows you to create spreadsheets. This program is great for tracking clients, lenders, and loans.

- Access is a database program. Creating a database of clients makes it easy to organize information. You can also create a database with potential borrowers and leads. A separate one can be created for lenders.

Using the Internet

The Internet has expanded the marketing opportunities for mortgage brokers. A Web site allows you to reach a far greater number of clients than you would by relying only on offline marketing and advertising methods. Building a Web site and working on increasing your ranking in the search engines is a good way to reach out to potential clients and build your business.

The Internet has made communication with borrowers, potential clients, and lenders faster and easier. You can utilize e-mail for marketing as well as communication. E-mail marketing campaigns are faster and less expensive than direct mail. A well-crafted e-mail campaign is a great way to target new borrowers.

When crafting your e-mail, use success stories from the past and former clients' testimonials. This gives you more credibility as a mortgage broker and will help to increase your response. Describe a particularly problematic loan. What was the problem? How did your expertise help to solve the problem for the borrower? Using personal stories in your e-mail marketing is a good way to illustrate the unique services you offer.

Be sure to be unique in your e-mail communications. When potential borrowers have been searching the Internet for a loan, they will most likely be getting e-mail communications from several brokers. Make yours stand out from the pack. Rather than using standard lines about what a broker does or how having a broker will benefit the client, highlight your specific expertise and past success. This will help you stand out from the other mortgage brokers and lenders the potential client is considering.

One thing that will help you stand out from other mortgage brokers is your response time. The faster you can respond to inquiries and questions from clients and potential clients, the faster you build a reputation as a professional. E-mail communication and a good Web site will help your clients get their inquiries answered faster, which will increase the chance that they will use your service and then refer their friends and family to you.

Include all information for your Web site and e-mail address in all of your written and e-mail communications. Another idea is to include the information in your voice mail message. If potential clients are looking for information, they can visit your Web site. This way they get some information quickly while waiting for a call back. This can make the difference between the borrower waiting for that return call or just going on to the next broker on their list.

Online Tools and Ideas

Including tools and calculators on your Web site is a good way to help clients and bring visitors back to your site. If they find useful information and can make calculations related to their situation, they will come back to use them again. Some good tools to include on your site include mortgage calculators, refinancing calculators, payment calculators, and renting vs. owning comparisons.

When you are building your Web site, include an option that allows clients to check the status of their application online. This will allow clients to access this information without having to place a call to your office. Clients like this feature and it may result in fewer phone calls for you to return.

Be sure to keep your Web site up to date with current interest rates. These change frequently so you will need to stay on top of this. When customers hear on the morning news that the Fed is lowering interest rates, they tend to head to the Internet to compare rates. If the information on your Web site is not up to date, the customer will go looking elsewhere for lower rates and updated information. Do not let this happen to you. It can cut into your income.

Include options for clients to communicate with you via the Web site. Once they see your site and are considering doing business with you, they will want to make contact quickly. Include a link to your e-mail so they can click the link to send an e-mail. Some sites allow customers to fill out a form to get more information on home loans or to contact you.

Internet Leads

The Internet offers several opportunities for generating leads and finding new clients. A Web site is a good place to start, but will not be enough to grow your business. You will need other sources for finding new clients. The reason your own Web site will not be sufficient lies in search engine marketing. The top spots in the search engines are reserved for companies that pay big bucks to get there.

If your site is not in the top page or two on the search engine, you will not get enough attention from people searching for mortgage brokers. Most people do not make it past the first one to three pages on an Internet search. As a result, a broker that is listed on page three or four on the search engine will not generate enough new leads to stay in business and become successful.

To help generate business, consider getting listed in some of the mortgage broker directories on the Internet. There are several Web sites that offer directories with listings of mortgage brokers. Adding your company to that list can help bring prospective borrowers to you. Some of these directories are free of charge, but others charge an annual fee for the service.

In some cases, you need to join the site or organization to be listed in the directory. An example of this is the National Association of Mortgage Brokers (NAMB) Web site. The brokers listed in the directory on that Web site are members of NAMB. Getting listed on the site is just one more reason brokers may want to consider membership in this professional organization.

A big benefit of getting listed in mortgage broker directories is that these large sites do have a high ranking in the search engine. The company or organization has paid the big money required for that ranking. You can take advantage of this by being listed on these sites. The fee you pay to belong will be far less than you would pay to get your site listed near the top of the rankings.

Web Sites That Offer Mortgage Broker Directories

- **www.best-mortgage-lender.us**
- **www.mortgage-broker-directory.us**
- **www.home-mortgage-brokers.us**
- **www.bad-credit-mortgage-lenders.us**
- **www.mortgage-loan-broker.us**
- **www.mortgage-loan-online.us**
- **www.mortgage-refinance-company.us**
- **www.lender411.com**

Some Web sites are dedicated to providing solid mortgage leads to brokers. These sites charge a fee for these leads. The benefit is that the leads are solid and likely to result in loan closings. These lead-generating companies are different from the lists of names you can purchase from some companies for marketing purposes. Those lists are not filtered and have not been contacted to determine if they are interested in a new mortgage or to refinance an existing home loan.

Good lead-generating companies will take the list and eliminate any leads that are found to be bogus. The leads that you receive will have been filtered according to the criteria you select. This criterion can be general or to a more specific niche market, such as refinancing, poor credit loans, or commercial. You will get leads targeted to your business that are likely to result in closed loans.

You will need to pay for the services offered by these companies. The fee depends on the number of leads and the individual company. Prices can range into the thousands of dollars, depending on the package you select. Some companies will guarantee a minimum number of loans that will go to closing with these packages, so you are not gambling with your hard-earned money. For example, some will have a set number, such as 20 loans per month.

Some offer leads by live transfer. A representative of the loan-generation company will do the cold calling and locate interested borrowers. When the borrowers are found, the company will transfer the call to your phone. This is done in real time and the borrower gets to speak to a mortgage broker right away to have his questions answered and discuss his situation with you.

As with any service provider you would use for your business, check out the-lead generating company before forking over thousands of dollars. Ask questions before committing to any service.Examples of questions to ask include:

- How long has the company been in business?
- How many mortgage brokers use the service?
- How many guaranteed leads you will get each month based on the package you choose?
- What happens if you do not get the minimum number of leads in a given month or over the course of a few months?
- What is the company's ratio of leads to credit reports pulled? In other words, of the number of leads they pass on, what percentage goes on to have the mortgage broker pull the credit report and get the ball rolling for a mortgage?

Ask other brokers about the companies they use to generate leads. Some may not share this information readily, since they will view you as the competition. If you are part of an online forum or professional organization, ask the members of these groups for their input. The people that are in your group will not all live and work in your general area. As a result, they are less likely to see you as a source of competition and more likely to offer a recommendation and other assistance.

Marketing Technology and Tips

Another way to use the Internet to generate and manage leads is the lead call capturing system of marketing. These companies help you generate leads and provide your prospective borrowers with information at any time of the day or night. This system is used in conjunction with other advertising and marketing that you do both online and offline. The company has a nationwide toll free number that is known as a vanity number.

You include this general toll free number in all your advertising along with a numeric code for your prospective clients to enter when they call. The automated service will pick up the call and ask the caller to enter the code. This code is assigned to your specific business, so all calls with your code will be forwarded to you without fear of duplication with other brokers.

Once the potential client enters the code, he will hear your voice mail message. A menu follows with touch-tone options for the client to choose from. Some of these options include leaving a voice mail and requesting that information on loans be sent via fax or e-mail. The people that are answering your ads will follow the prompt to get the information they require or to leave a message for you.

You have some options regarding how these calls are managed after they are received. Some brokers opt to have the calls transferred to their phones. Others utilize the voice messaging that is offered by the company or have the calls transferred and then let the voice mail pick it up. These numbers can be changed via the Web site as needed. For example, say you are having the calls transferred to your office phone. If you will be out of the office, you can change your settings to have the calls sent to your cell phone or home.

Most companies offer solutions for you to monitor the progress and leads generated. In most cases, this can be done online. You can manage your account online and even listen to your messages via the Web site to save you time and money since you will not have to phone in every time you want to manage your account. A good site will offer detailed instructions, online tutorials, and tech support for new users to learn to navigate the call management system.

A great feature of these services is the ability to generate reports. You can read the call reports on the Internet. The reports are available with a variety of options, including information on where the call was placed. A report can be generated to determine where the calls are originating. This will help you make decisions regarding future advertising. You will have all the information you need to determine which advertising campaigns are brining results and which are not. Since the advertising budgets of most brokers are not very large, this is a great added benefit of these services.

The cost varies according to several factors. Some companies charge a flat fee for the service and others charge per call. Which payment method is most beneficial for your business will often depend on how many calls are generated and transferred through the site. Some offer packages with an overall price for a predetermined number of minutes. The price for these packages will depend on the number of minutes built into the contract. Often, these are more minutes than are needed.

Other services offer pricing per minute. With this method, you are only paying for the minutes you use each month. The number of minutes you use each month will vary, but you are only paying for what you are using. This can save a lot of money, especially for a new broker who has not yet built up the business enough to use the service a lot. In this case, the pay-per-minute package is the best option. If the firm is busy and gets a large number of calls, the overall package of minutes may work out to cost less.

CHAPTER 16

Tips for Success

Sharpen your sales skills: Never forget that when you work as a mortgage broker, you are in sales. You are not selling mortgage products or even interest rates; you are selling yourself and your services. Read about sales techniques used by the best in the business. Learn from these techniques and use them to increase your success in the mortgage broker business.

Use your sphere of influence: This is all the people in your life. Remember the database or list you made of all the people in your life? Add to this list all the time. These people are a great continual source of referrals. Be sure to cultivate this source and use your existing relationships to get your business off the ground and keep it going.

Make cold calls: There will be some cold calling involved in your business. Whether these are leads you purchase or get from a professional, you will need to make that first call to establish contact with the potential borrower. No one likes to make cold calls, but it can be a successful method of generating business. The best way to get over a fear of or aversion to cold calling is to just do it. Over time you will get better at it, although you may never like it.

Build relationships: When you are joining professional organizations or connecting with professionals to seek referrals, avoid centering all the conversation on you and your business. Get to know people on a more personal level. People refer their clients to professionals they like. The time you spend in building these relationships will pay off in more loan closings in the future.

Attitude is everything: Your skills, education, and experience look great on your resume, but is it enough to ensure success? In the end, people do business with brokers for their personality as much as their experience. A friendly, outgoing attitude will do wonders to increase your success. Always keep a positive attitude, even in difficult situations.

Never stop learning: In the beginning of your career, you will spend a lot of time learning about the mortgage business. Your education should not end with your licensing. It also should not be restricted to the number of hours required for license renewal. Your education should be an ongoing process. There are always changes in the mortgage industry and you want to remain on the cutting edge of these changes and developments. The best way to do this is to continually increase your education and never stop learning.

Mistakes New Brokers Make

Any professional new to any industry will make mistakes in the beginning. There is a learning curve with any new career and mortgage brokers are no exception. Fortunately you do not have to make all these mistakes to learn from them. You can learn from the early mistakes of other new brokers.

Failing to protect the personal information of clients: Over the past several years, there have been a few news stories about sensitive documents being thrown in dumpsters behind brokerage firms. The danger of this practice is the potential for identity theft. Documents related to home loans contain all the information an unscrupulous person would need to assume the identity of your clients and go on a major spending spree.

As a broker, it is your responsibility to protect the personal information of your clients and past clients. Old files should never be thrown in a dumpster where they could be retrieved by someone else. If you are purging your files, be sure to shred all the documents first. This will prevent the danger of your client's sensitive personal information from being stolen on your watch.

In some states, the practice of disposing of this information without shredding is against the law. In 2005, a mortgage broker in Honolulu was fined $10,000 when a newspaper reporter found boxes of files dumped without being shredded. The ensuing story got the attention of the state's attorney general and the company was fined. This is becoming standard practice in other areas of the country as well.

Not doing credit rescoring: Credit rescoring is done by companies that specialize in rapid credit rescoring. This is not something your borrowers can do for themselves. Only a mortgage broker or lender has access to these companies. Since you have access as a professional, this can be a great benefit to your clients. Some brokers shy away from rescoring because it takes time and costs some money.

How does credit rescoring work? Say you have a client that has negative items on his credit report that are either mistakes or the result of identity theft. The client could contact the credit bureau and dispute the incorrect items listed on the report. The credit bureau must investigate and remove the information that is not accurate. However, this takes time, often a month or more. In the meantime, the client could lose a good deal on a mortgage or end up paying a higher interest rate.

With rapid rescoring, the mortgage broker contacts the credit bureau to have the items removed from the report. This is done right away by the rescoring company and then the credit score is recalculated. The new score will be higher, which will result in a better deal on a home loan. Over the life of the loan, the difference is often in the tens of thousands of dollars.

From time to time, a savvy borrower may know about credit rescoring and may ask you about the possibility of using this method to improve the credit score. It is important to help the client understand the accounts that qualify and do not qualify for rescoring. This can only be done for incorrect entries or when the creditor agrees to remove the item. The borrower will need to provide some type of proof that the account information is not correct in order to have it removed from the report.

Thinking deals will just come to them: This is one of the biggest mistake new mortgage brokers make when starting out in business. Deals will not just come to you, even in the best of times. You need to get out there and continually work for them. This is the best way to ensure success in your new business.

Underestimating the start-up costs of business: This mistake is not limited to mortgage brokers. Professionals in many industries tend to underestimate how much money will be needed to get a business started and actually turning a profit. In addition to your start-up costs, you need to have some money in the bank to keep the business going long enough to experience success.

You should have at least a few months' worth of bill money in the bank to pay the bills for your business as well as your personal bills. When you are making a budget for start-up costs, add a cushion into the budget. This will allow extra money for the unexpected expenses that always seem to crop up when starting out in business.

A lack of goals or a marketing plan: Some brokers start out with a vague idea or an overall plan, but lack specific goals and objectives for achieving success. Take the time to write complete, specific, and measurable goals for your business. Re-evaluate these goals on a regular basis and make the necessary changes. The same is true for your marketing plan. You need a well-thought-out plan for marketing your business. You should track the success of your plan, evaluate it, and make changes on a regular basis.

HOUSE

CHAPTER

17

Surviving When Business Is Slow

When you are working in the home-lending industry, there are slow times and busy times. This goes with the territory. When the market and interest rates are favorable, more people will be looking to purchase or refinance homes. This is a great time to be a broker and there is plenty of money to be made. However, it will not last. What goes up will eventually come down. This is true for the housing market.

When the market is slow, the economy is not great, or interest rates are not so favorable, there will be fewer people in the market for a new home. There will also be a smaller pool of homeowners that are interested in refinancing their homes. Recent problems in the subprime market appear to be extending into the rest of the mortgage industry.

This is likely to result in changes for mortgage brokers. Lenders are getting tougher on loan approvals in light of recent developments within the industry. People that may have qualified for a subprime loan a few short years ago may be turned away. This presents additional challenges for the mortgage broker in locating programs and preparing convincing application packages.

It is during these more difficult economic times that many brokers end up closing their doors. The successful mortgage broker is able to continue to thrive when the market takes a turn. So, how can your business survive the slow times, so yours will not be one of the brokerage firms closing its doors?

There are several things you can do to make it through the tough times. A smart way to start is by planning for the lean months. When the market is booming, either in new homes or refinancing, make wise financial decisions. You should be investing and saving a portion of that income to help make it through the lean times.

When the market is down, loans will not appear on your doorstep. While this is always true, it is especially true when the market is low. You will need to get out there and find work. Contact the past clients and professionals in your database to drum up new business. You will spend a larger portion of your time looking for new business in tough economic times.

Expand your reach for finding clients. If you have worked mostly with local builders, Realtors, and use mostly local professionals as a source of referrals, you need to reach out beyond your current boundaries. Consider obtaining a license for each of the states bordering the state where you are currently doing business. This will allow you to find clients in the surrounding areas which can help bring in additional business.

The Effect of the Economy

There is debate, even among economists, about the effect of the economy on the mortgage market. A sluggish economy or changes in interest rates do not always indicate trouble for the mortgage market. However, there are indicators that can signal trouble coming in the future for the economy.

Economic Indicators to Watch

Economists analyze certain indictors to determine the state of the economy. A bad sign in one of these indicators does not necessarily signify a recession. However, bad news from a few segments of the economy can spell trouble on the horizon. When you are informed about these economic indicators and follow news stories in print publications and on news programs, you will be in a better position to not only help your clients, but protect your business as well.

Employment

It seems obvious for employment to be an economic indicator to watch. When the economy takes a downward turn, there is often job loss. When the job loss is large enough, there will be an effect on the mortgage market. Fewer employed people translate into fewer borrowers for home loans. In addition, there will not be as many people interested in refinancing their homes.

The employment figures you hear on television and read in the newspaper come from the federal government. The government conducts a survey each month of American business and employment rates. This survey measures both new jobs created and the unemployment rate.

What economists and mortgage brokers want to see is an employment report that shows both a low rate of unemployment and growth in the job creation figures. When people are gainfully employed and experiencing a period of job security, they tend to purchase homes. This employment situation combined with falling interest rates is great for the refinance market and second mortgages.

The Consumer Price Index (CPI) tracks spending patterns in the United States. These calculations are performed by the Bureau of Labor Statistics every year to determine the costs of various goods and services. The spending categories of two groups of people are used to calculate the Consumer Price Index: urban consumers and urban wage earners.

Urban consumers is a broad category, which includes a wide range of people from professionals to unemployed and retired people. These are people that live within urban areas and is said to account for over 80 percent of the population of the United States. This group is considered to be a more reliable measure because it is a higher percentage of the general public.

The other group used to calculate the Consumer Price Index is urban wage earners. This group includes people working in clerical, sales, and craft jobs as well as service workers and laborers.

The prices of a variety of expenses are included in the Consumer Price Index. These include the prices of housing, transportation, medical care, education, clothing, and other common household goods. Information on the current expenditures in these categories are referenced to data from the mid-1980s. The index shows an increase or decrease in prices.

The CPI is one indicator of economic trends in the United States. Large changes in prices in a short period of time, either an increase or a decrease, are a sign of inflation or deflation. The CPI is considered one of the most reliable measures of inflation. It is one of the factors economists look at when analyzing the economy.

The CPI offers useful information to the mortgage broker. The reports on housing costs give a picture of the health of the housing market. Ideally, prices should be increasing, not decreasing, but not to the point of inflation. During periods of inflation, interest rates will increase. If rates increase significantly, this can affect your business. Fewer people refinance homes when interest rates increase.

The Stock Market

As a mortgage broker, you may not think the stock market is something you need to watch. This is not true, particularly if you are interested in watching economic factors that have an impact on your business. Certain indicators from the stock market can give insight into the health of the mortgage and housing markets.

The stock market affects interest rates and this affects your business. Mortgages are sold on the stock market as mortgage-backed securities. This market has an effect on interest rates. Interest rates tend to rise as the market prices on mortgage bonds fall. The yield rate on the securities has to rise. This attracts investors to mortgaged-backed securities, which results in more money invested. The downside is that interest rates will go up to compensate for the higher yield.

The Federal Reserve

The Federal Reserve is the central system of banks in the United

States. The system is part government and part private. The Fed was created in 1913 as a response to fiscal crises and "bank runs." Public panics resulting in customers lining up to take their money from the banks is an image we associate with the crash of 1929. In fact, these bank runs happened frequently enough to cause serious concern in Washington. After a large bank run in 1907, the Federal Reserve was formed.

The role of the Federal Reserve has grown and evolved since its inception. The Fed now regulates the money supply in the country, buys and sells securities, and lends money to commercial banks in the United States. The Fed also sets the discount interest rate. This is the rate the Federal Reserve charges banks for borrowing money.

Several factors influence the discount rate. The discount rate does not always have a direct effect on the rates your clients will get on their loans. If the Fed cuts the discount rate by a quarter of 1 percent, this will not necessarily result in a quarter of 1 percent drop in your client's rate. However, the discount rate does affect the general range of prime loans. When the discount rate is lower, rates on these loans tend to be more favorable. The best situation for a low rate is a growing economy with no inflation. When prices are inflated, interest rates get higher.

The National and Local Real Estate Markets

The mortgage broker's business is dependent on clients buying and selling homes. Therefore, the housing market is one portion of the economy you should continue to watch. The information on housing starts and sales of existing homes reported on CNN and other news programs are national figures. These indicate the overall changes in the housing market in the whole country.

This is only part of the picture. The local housing market is the one that will most affect your business. This is the housing market in your state and neighboring states, if you do business there. The national housing market may be an indication of the market in your area, but this is not always the case.

When the national housing market is down, there are still pockets throughout the country where real estate is booming. You may be lucky enough to live and work in one of these areas. The opposite can also be true. Some areas may experience an economic downturn or a slow housing market at a time when the numbers in the country as a whole are looking pretty good.

The local real estate market affects your business in a few different ways. When the market is good, there are plenty of borrowers looking for a mortgage. However, when the local housing market is flat or in decline, there is less work to be found. It is during these times the broker needs to work harder to find business.

A slow or declining housing market can also affect the appraisals on properties your borrowers are hoping to finance. When the market is in decline, prices begin to fall. This can reduce the appraised value of properties, which causes problems with the lender. It may be harder for your client to meet the lender's requirements for loan-to-value-ratio when the appraisal comes in low.

You can anticipate this by learning about appraisals and paying attention to changes in appraisal values in your local market. As you spend time doing this, you will increase your knowledge of appraisals. You will actually begin to predict the appraisal value before you have the report in your hands. This will allow you to predict problems and assist your clients.

Growing Your Business in a Slow Market

When the market slows, you will spend even more time than usual in attracting new business. Start by revising the short-term goals for your business. You may have to change or rewrite some of your goals to work for your current situation. Rewriting your goals is a great motivator when times are tough.

Next, evaluate your marketing campaign. What have you been doing to attract business? Which methods have been working and which have not brought much, or any, new clients to your door? Since you will be working with a smaller budget in a slow market, it is more important than ever to invest your money wisely in terms of advertising or generating leads.

If you have additional time on your hands, now may be a good time to increase your education. Take some workshops related to the mortgage or real estate industries. You can take classes at a local college or university which can be used as credits toward a graduate degree.

There are also workshops in state mortgage broker associations or through the National Association of Mortgage Brokers. Some of these are offered in a traditional classroom format and others are offered entirely online. These are a great option for the busy professional working hard to grow and maintain a business.

CHAPTER

18

Case Studies

Case Study: Ken Lambert

Ken Lambert

Senior Mortgage Consultant

Qualified Mortgage Solutions

Brentwood, NH

Direct line: 978-764-8470

Web site - **www.homequitybuilder.info**

Blog - **http://homequitybuilder.mortgagefit.com**

How did you get started as a mortgage broker?

I worked for 2 different real estate developers, where I was in charge of construction loans as well as our own real estate sales at the closings. I learned all about the mortgage process at that time, as far as preparing for closings (appraisals, insurance forms, HUD settlement statements, and so on). Then I started working as a PT loan officer for a mortgage brokerage firm.

What training or education have you had?

The first brokerage that I worked for trained me in-house, via classes and also their training manual/binder. Other than that, I conducted much of my own mortgage business research during my development of a new (and patent-pending) mortgage loan product.

How do you use technology in your business?

I use the Internet all the time — going onto wholesale lenders' Web sites where we log in to view all their loan programs and rate sheets. I've also used Calyx Point

Case Study: Ken Lambert

software, which is the largest loan operating system being used out in the market. And of course e-mail is the preferred method for many people (including buyers/clients) for communication and electronic document transferals.

Do you have a niche market for finding clients?

I am the regional sales representative for a niche company called **CheapHousePayments.com**. This association has given me a few leads, as has being involved in an online mortgage community called **www.mortgagefit.com**.

What professional organizations do you belong to? How have these memberships helped you achieve success?

I am a member of MBARL (Mortgage Brokers Association for Responsible Lending). It is a good thing to put on my business cards and other forms of advertising. Anything to try to set yourself apart from all the other mortgage professionals out there is helpful.

Tell me a little about your business, loan volume, number of employees, any other relevant information.

I work for a company called Qualified Mortgage Solutions, a small brokerage owned by two partners, with a total of six loan officers and one and a half loan processors. The company is licensed in Massachusetts and New Hampshire. As an office, we close between 12 and 20 loans per month, in the current market. We have four full-time loan officers, and two part-time officers.

What are some successful methods you use to generate leads?

As mentioned above, I do get some leads via those two affiliations. Other than that, I do make telemarketing calls to people that took out adjustable-rate mortgages over the last three years. The office buys these nonexclusive leads for us, the loan officers. We have to make the calls and set the appointments, etc. In addition, I try to network with local real estate agents — mainly from smaller or independent real estate agencies.

Do you work for a company or are you self-employed? Why did you make this choice?

I work for a company. I chose this because I still needed some professional seasoning and guidance. I did not have enough experience to set out on my own as a separate company or as a branch manager for a net branch of a national company. Also, I don't have to worry much about all the compliance and regulatory issues. The back office and owner handle that load.

Case Study: Ken Lambert

What type of advertising do you do? What has been most successful for generating new business?

We conduct home buyer seminars every month or two — and not just first-time buyer seminars. We also have a niche market in the REO and foreclosed properties. We have found that postcard mailings are generally NOT worth the money that we spend for them. We also will post newspaper advertisements every few months in some of the local newspapers to help get the word out about our company and our name.

Any tips for establishing a good relationship with lenders?

Just be sincere and up front with those lender account executives, as you would with anyone in business. And do your homework regarding the loan programs they offer before asking them a bunch of "dumb" questions. It does not make you look very professional.

Tips for finding the best deals for your clients:

Make your own calls and check out your key lender's Web sites and rate sheets. But also ask other more senior loan officers in your office as to what they would do and who they would try. Everyone has a little different knowledge and has their own expertise.

Tips for putting together a loan package:

Always use a checklist, especially if you are starting out in the business. And with some of the more paperwork-heavy programs, you should compile a cheat sheet of what you will need from the buyer. It does not look very good if you have to go back two or three times. Plus it will delay the underwriting and the closing.

Tips for success as a mortgage broker:

Be willing to make some cold calls, and be willing to work the various lead sheets that you may get or purchase. Join local business organizations just to get your name and business card out in the local community. Make sure you let everyone in your sphere of influence (friends, neighbors, relatives, etc.) know that you are in the mortgage business, and you will get a few calls/loans per year just by default.

What are some pitfalls for new brokers to avoid, or some common mistakes made by new brokers?

Most assume that it will be easy money and easy living. For some people it might be, but that is usually after being in the business for numerous years and having plenty of referral and repeat customers. It will take you two to three years just to get to that

Case Study: Ken Lambert

point of full-time work. A lot of new brokers start out in a part-time manner because they cannot guarantee themselves a satisfactory income as they are spreading their name and learning the business.

What would you say is the biggest mistake new brokers make when they are starting out?

They think that deals will fall into their laps. That almost never happens from my experience. Even if you have a referral customer, they will be shopping your rates and fees with at least one other broker or lender, so you still have competition and have to earn their business.

Any other advice?

Being a mortgage broker is not for everyone. It is very sales oriented, so if you are not a salesperson or if you are not comfortable in the public or trying to make a sales pitch to neighbors, then it might not be for you. People don't buy anything from people who they do not like, so it's best to have a good attitude and be likeable/sociable.

Case Study: Jerry Cox

Jerry Cox

President

Heritage Mortgage

2565 Barrington Circle

Tallahassee, FL 32308

850-531-9995 Office

850-445-3188 Cell

850-531-9940 Fax

How did you get started as a mortgage broker?

I began my lending career employed by a state-chartered bank.

What training or education have you had?

I hold a CRMS CRS degree plus hundreds of technical hours of formal training.

How do you use technology in your business?

In every aspect: ordering, ADM, underwriting, and closing.

Case Study: Jerry Cox

Do you have a niche market for finding clients?

Niche has gone away for the most part. Although there is always going to be a demand for specialization.

What professional organizations do you belong to? How have these memberships helped you achieve success?

Florida Association of Mortgage Brokers, the National Association of Mortgage Brokers. Both have done a fairly good job of lobbying as well as training.

Tell me a little about your business: loan volume, number of employees, and any other relevant information.

At one time, I employed as many as 24 employees. Our annual dollar volume has been in excess of $45 million annually.

What are some successful methods you use to generate leads?

Television and word of mouth.

Do you work for a company or are you self-employed? Why did you make this choice?

Self-employed. Most mortgage broker business is mismanaged and run without true direction.

What type of advertising do you do? What has been most successful for generating new business?

Word of mouth and referrals.

Tips for establishing a good relationship with lenders:

Most lenders have less integrity than mortgage brokers. You as a broker must guard your business and manage your relationship.

Tips for finding the best deals for your clients:

Develop multiple relationships and deep interviewing of your client to profile your client's needs and short- and long-term goals.

Tips for putting together a loan package:

Hire a staff or team dedicated to this discipline.

Case Study: Jerry Cox

Tips for success as a mortgage broker:

Education. Listen to your client. Always do the right thing, even if it does not benefit you as the broker.

What are some pitfalls for new brokers to avoid, or some common mistakes made by new brokers?

Trusting your lender representative. They tend to overstate the company's position. Reverify programs.

What would you say is the biggest mistake new brokers make when they are starting out?

Underfunding start-up costs. Either as a broker or an owner. Poor marketing plans, if they even have a plan.

Any other advice?

Work for a professional broker for at least three years. Understand the laws and rules of the trade. Never overstate what you can do as a broker.

Case Study: Darryl Crawford

Darryl Crawford

Your Personal Mortgage Consultant

AMC Mortgage, LLC

205 Wild Basin Rd., Bldg. 3, #200

Austin, TX 78746

512-394-0111 office

512-394-0112 fax

512-517-7816 cell

TX MB License #33717

How did you get started as a mortgage broker?

My family started the business in 1992 in Bryan, Texas.

What training or education have you had?

Case Study: Darryl Crawford

At the time I entered the industry there was very little training available. Since Texas instituted licensing for mortgage brokers in 2001, I have received over 120 hours of CE. Mostly, the "school of hard knocks" has taught us what to do as a company.

How do you use technology in your business?

We have gone from taking handwritten loan applications to a fully automated, online system. Software programs such as Calyx Point have become standard operating procedure in our daily operations. Voice mail, e-mail, market tracking, and a Web site to obtain new customers all fit within our business plan.

Do you have a niche market for finding clients?

We've specialized in construction financing for single-family residences for the past ten years. Relationships with builders have been our largest lead-generation point.

What professional organizations do you belong to? How have these memberships helped you achieve success?

As a CEO as well as a mortgage broker, being affiliated with organizations within the industry is key to our success. We belong to both NAMB and TAMB, as well as the chamber of commerce, BBB, and I am personally a member in a CEO group named Vistage. Not only does belonging add credibility to our business, these affiliations allow us to work on our industry, as well as in it.

Tell me a little about your business: loan volume, number of employees, and any other relevant information.

In 2006 we closed $108 million in total volume. This was a mix of one-time-close construction loans, purchases of conventional and FHA, as well as refinances. We are a full-service company with ten loan officers, two processors, and an admin. We are based in Austin with branch offices in Houston, Dallas, San Antonio, and Bastrop.

What are some successful methods you use to generate leads?

We are a by-referral company that prefers to use our past client base to generate future business. Our loan officers are trained as street solicitors, rather than relying on purchased leads or ABA agreements with real estate companies.

Do you work for a company or are you self-employed? Why?

I am one of two owners of AMC Mortgage. My business partner, Jake Costin, is also my brother-in-law. We prefer to be self-employed, and teach our employees the principles of working for themselves.

Case Study: Darryl Crawford

What type of advertising do you do? What has been most successful for generating new business?

We do not advertise.

Tips for establishing a good relationship with lenders:

Honesty and education. If you lie to a lender, there will be no trust. Without trust there is no relationship. If you "learn your craft," you will find the right way to close a loan every time.

Tips for finding the best deals for your clients:

It is imperative that you understand your client's needs, before deciding on what the best options will be. How long will they live there? What other investments do they have? Can they afford what they want? The answers to these questions are the cornerstone to placing them in the best product.

Tips for putting together a loan package:

Tell a story. Make sure that the package explains the client's "story" before you submit it. Tell the underwriter what you are trying to accomplish, and then leave a trail of bread crumbs through the file, by marking or labeling every exhibit.

Tips for success as a mortgage broker:

Build long-lasting relationships with your employees, referral sources and lenders. Show up on time. Be professional. Always have your client's interest ahead of your own. Educate yourself at every opportunity, and share that knowledge with everyone in your industry.

What are some pitfalls for new brokers to avoid, or some common mistakes made by new brokers?

Hit the streets running. Do not buy leads, or spend thousands of dollars on mail-outs for a 2 percent return. People do business with people they like and trust. That cannot be accomplished through an e-mail or mail-out. Dress professionally. Notify clients immediately upon an issue arising, and address it with solutions. Hiding the truth hurts everyone. (I call this, "If you have to eat a turd, don't nibble at it!")

What would you say is the biggest mistake new brokers make when they are starting out?

They wait for business to come to them, rather than going out and finding it.

Case Study: Darryl Crawford

Any other advice?

The mortgage industry is a wonderful place to make a living. You can help someone buy their first home, help them finance college for their children, and help them find their piece of the American Dream.

If you want to enter this industry, decide who the first 100 people you will tell about it are, and call them. Be prepared to live for three months without a paycheck. Expensive office space never made money for anyone but the landlord. Jeans are for riding horses or wearing to the movies; they have no place in the office. If you say it, do it. Never let your alligator mouth overload your hummingbird ass. (I am from Texas; I thought you might appreciate a little colloquialism.)

APPENDIX

Licensing Requirements by State

Alabama

State of Alabama
Banking Department
PO Box 4600
Montgomery, AL 36103-4600
Phone: 334-242-3452
Web site: **www.banking.alabama.gov/Applications/bol_applications_ambla.htm**

Licensing Fee: $500 and $100 for background investigation

Additional Requirements: Must complete 12 hours of continuing education. Three letters of reference are needed from lenders and three from community members. A copy of the customer-broker agreement and articles of incorporation are also required.

Alaska

Alaska Division of Banking
Securities and Corporations
PO Box 110807
Juneau, AK 99881-0807
Phone: 907-465-2521
Web site: **www.commerce.state.ak.us/occ/mortgagelicensing/index.htm**

Licensing Fee: $500 biannual fee and $250 application and background investigation fee

Additional Requirements: Alaska will begin requiring licensing for mortgage brokers on July 1, 2008. A background investigation including fingerprinting and a passing score on the state exam are required. A surety bond is needed. Also, 24 hours of continuing education will be needed every two years for license renewal.

Arkansas

Arkansas Securities Department
Heritage West Building, Suite 300
201 East Markham Street
Little Rock, AK 72201-1692
Phone: 501-324-9260
Web site: **www.securities.arkansas.gov/Securities_Section/bd_firm.html**

Licensing Fee: $750

Additional Requirements: Surety bond, minimum of three years of experience in mortgage lending, audited financial statements, and a minimum net worth of $25,000.

Arizona

Arizona Department of Financial Institutions
2910 N 44th Street, Suite 310
Phoenix, AZ 85018
Phone: 602-255-4421 or 800-544-0708
Web site: **www.azdfi.gov**

Licensing Fee: $800

Additional Requirements: Broker must maintain a physical office in the state of Arizona. Applicants must have three years' experience, attend a mortgage broker school, and pass the required exam. Fingerprints and a surety bond are also required.

California

Department of Corporations
320 West 4th Street, Suite 750
Los Angeles, CA 90013-1105
Phone: 213-576-7500
Web site: **www.corp.ca.gov**

Licensing Fee: $200 certificate fee and $100 investigation fee

Additional Requirements: Applicants must pass a written exam and need to successfully complete two college level courses and 45 hours of continuing education. Broker must maintain an office within the state of California and have two years of experience in the mortgage or real estate industry. A surety bond is required.

Colorado

Department of Regulatory Agencies
Division of Real Estate
1560 Broadway, Suite 925
Denver, CO 80202
Phone: 303-9-894-2166
Web site: **www.dora.state.co.us/real-estate/mortgagebrokerregistration.htm**

Licensing Fee: No license is required, but a $200 registration fee is required

Additional Requirements: Criminal background check and surety bond are required. There are no education requirements and no exam.

Connecticut

Department of Banking
260 Constitution Plaza
Hartford, CT 03103-1800
Phone: 860-240-8299
Web site: **www.ct.gov/dob**

Licensing Fee: $400 each for first and second mortgage licenses

Additional Requirements: There are separate licenses for first and second mortgages. To hold both licenses, applicant must have three years of supervisory experience in the last five years. A surety bond, net worth of $25,000, and audited financial statements are required.

Delaware

Office of State Banking Commissioner
555 E Loockerman Street, Suite 210
Dover, DE 19901
Phone: 302-739-4235
Web site: **www.banking.delaware.gov/services/applicense/applyfor.shtml**

Licensing Fee: $250 license fee and $250 fee for background investigation

Additional Requirements: Three letters of reference from companies doing business with broker and surety bond.

Florida

Department of Securities and Finance
200 E Gaines Street
Tallahassee, FL 32399
Phone: 850-410-9805
Web site: **www.flofr.com/licensing**

Licensing Fees: $200 licensing fee and $23 for fingerprinting

Additional requirements: Must take 24 hours of instruction and pass the state exam to be licensed as a mortgage broker. A background investigation including fingerprinting is required.

Georgia

Georgia Department of Banking and Finance
2990 Brandywine Road, Suite 200
Atlanta, GA 30341-5565
Phone: 770-986-1633
Web site: **http://dbf.georgia.gov**

Licensing Fees: $500 licensing fee and $250 background investigation fee

Additional Requirements: Applicants must complete 40 hours of education in mortgage education, of which four hours must be devoted to the Georgia Residential Mortgage Act. A surety bond and background investigation is required. Two years of prior experience in the mortgage industry is required.

Hawaii

Professional & Vocational Licensing Division
Department of Commerce and Consumer Affairs
PO Box 3469
Honolulu, HI 96801
Phone: 808-586-3000
Web site: **www.hawaii.gov/dcca/areas/pvl/programs/mortgage**

Licensing Fees: $320 in odd-numbered year, $185 in even-numbered year

Additional Requirements: Applicants must complete an 80-hour course and pass the exam. A minimum of three years' experience working with a professional broker is required. A physical office location within the state is required. Applicants must provide a surety bond and certified financial statements.

Idaho

Department of Finance
700 West State Street, 2nd Floor
Boise, ID 83720
Phone: 208-332-8000
Web site: **http://finance.idaho.gov/Mortgage/MortgageForms.aspx**

Licensing Fees: $350

Additional Requirements: There is no exam or educational requirements in Idaho. A surety bond is required. For office managers, three years of previous experience in the mortgage industry is required.

Illinois

Illinois Department of Financial and Professional Regulation
310 South Michigan, Suite 2130
Chicago, IL 60604-4278
Phone: 217-785-2903
Web site: **www.obre.state.il.us/RESFIN/Forms/rfformsb.htm**

Licensing Fees: $1,200 licensing fee and $1,500 background investigation fee are required annually.

Additional Requirements: A 30-hour education course or three years of experience and a written exam are required. Audited financial statements must be prepared within 90 days prior to the application date. In-state applicants must have a net worth of at least $50,000, for out-of-state applicants a net worth of $100,000 and a surety bond are required.

Indiana

Indiana Secretary of State
Securities Division
302 W. Washington Street, Room E - 111
Indianapolis, IN 46204
Phone: 317-232-6681
Web site: **www.in.gov/sos/securities**

Licensing Fee: $400

Additional Requirements: A background investigation and a surety bond are required. Applicants must complete a 24-hour educational course.

Iowa

Iowa Division of Banking
200 East Grand Avenue, Suite 300
Des Moines, IA 50309
Phone: 515-281-4014
Web site: **www.idob.state.ia.us**

Licensing Fee: $500

Additional Requirements: There is no exam or education requirement for mortgage brokers in Iowa. A surety bond is required and the broker must maintain a physical office within the state.

Kansas

Office of the State Bank Commissioner
700 SW Jackson Street, Suite 300
Topeka, KS 66603-3796
Phone: 785-296-2266
Web site: **www.osbckansas.org/DOCML/DOCMLApplications/docmlapplicationsmortgage.html**

Licensing Fees: $600 application fee and $54 fingerprint processing fee

Additional Requirements: Background investigation and surety bond.

Kentucky

Kentucky Office of Financial Institutions
1025 Capital Center Drive, Suite 200
Frankfort, KY 40601
Phone: 502-573-3390
Web site: **www.kfi.ky.gov**

Licensing Fees: $750

Additional Requirements: Current financial statements prepared by a certified public accountant. A 30-hour education course and a surety bond are required.

Louisiana

State of Louisiana
Office of Financial Institutions
8660 United Plaza Blvd, 2nd Floor
Baton Rouge, LA 70809
Phone: 225-925-4660
Web site: **www.ofi.state.la.us**

Licensing Fee: $45.25 for background investigation

Additional Requirements: Applicants must take a 10-hour educational course and pass the required exam. A surety bond or a net worth of at least $50,000 is required.

Maine

State of Maine
Bureau of Consumer Credit Protection
35 State House Station
Augusta, ME 04333-0035
Phone: 207-624-8527
Web site: **http://www.maine.gov/pfr/consumercredit/licensing/loan_broker/index.htm**

Licensing Fees: $400

Additional Requirements: Two professional letters of reference and a surety bond.

Maryland

Department of Labor, Licensing and Regulation
Commissioner of Financial Regulation
500 North Calvert Street, Suite 402
Baltimore, MD 21202
Phone: 410-230-6097
Web site: **www.dllr.state.md.us/finance**

Licensing Fees: $300 license fee and $100 investigation fee

Additional Requirements: Applicants are required to complete 40 hours of instruction and pass an exam. Three years of experience and a background investigation are required.

Massachusetts

Massachusetts Division of Banks
One South Station, 3rd Floor
Boston, MA 02110
Phone: 617-956-1500
Web site: **www.mass.gov/dob**

Licensing Fees: $1,000 fee on approval of application and $110 investigation fee

Additional Requirements: Surety bond, three professional letters of reference, and audited financial statements are required. As of November 1, 2007, Massachusetts uses the National Mortgage Licensing System.

Michigan

Mortgage and Consumer Finance Section
Attn: Licensing
PO Box 30220
Lansing, MI 48909
Phone: 877-999-6442
Web site: **www.michigan.gov/cis/0,1607,7-154-10555_22535_22536---,00.html**

Licensing Fees: $350 license fee and $450 investigation fee

Additional Requirements: A minimum net worth of $25,000, a surety bond, and financial statements are required. Applicant must attend a three-hour Mortgage Application Instructional Workshop.

Minnesota

Department of Commerce
Division of Financial Examinations
85 7th Place East, Suite 500
St Paul, MN 55101-2198
Phone: 651-282-9855
Web site: **http://www.state.mn.us/portal/mn/jsp/content.do?id=-536881352&agency=Commerce**

Licensing Fees: $1,000

Additional Information: A surety bond is required.

Mississippi

Department of Banking and Consumer Finance
901 Woolfolk Building Suite A
501 N West Street
Jackson, MS 39201
Phone: 601-359-1031
Web site: **www.dbcf.state.ms.us/loan_broker.htm**

Licensing Fees: $750

Additional Information: Applicant must either have two years of experience or pass an exam. The broker must maintain an office within the state. A background investigation and fingerprints, surety bond, and financial statements are required.

Missouri

Missouri Division of Finance
Harry S Truman State Office Building
PO Box 716
Jefferson City, MO 65102
Phone: 573-751-3242
Web site: **www.missouri-finance.org**

Licensing Fees: $300 licensing fee and $300 background investigation fee

Additional Information: A surety bond, financial statements, and a background investigation are required. The broker must maintain a physical office in the state.

Montana

Montana Department of Administration
Banking and Financial Institutions Division
301 South Park, Suite 316
Helena, MT 59620
Phone: 406-841-2920
Web site: **www.banking.mt.gov/mortgage.asp**

Licensing Fees: $500 and $29.25 fingerprinting fee

Additional Information: Three years of experience as a loan originator and an exam are required. A surety bond and a background investigation are required. The broker must maintain a physical office in the state of Montana.

Nebraska

Department of Banking & Finance
1230 O Street
Lincoln, NE 68508-1402
Phone: 402-471-2171
Web site: **www.ndbf.org/mb/mblicense.shtml**

Licensing Fees: $400

Additional Information: A surety bond and financial statements are required.

Nevada

400 W King Street, Suite 101
Carson City, NV 89703
Phone: 775-684-7060
Web site: **www.mld.nv.gov**

Licensing Fees: $1500

Additional Information: Financial statements for the past two years, a business plan, and a background investigation are required. Broker must have a physical office in the state.

New Hampshire

State of New Hampshire Banking Department
64B Old Suncook Road
Concord, NH 03301
Phone: 603-271-3561
Web site: **www.nh.gov/banking**

Licensing Fees: $500

Additional Information: A surety bond and background investigation are required.

New Jersey

New Jersey Department of Banking and Insurance
PO Box 325
Trenton, NJ 08625-0325
Phone: 609-292-5340
Web site: **www.state.nj.us/dobi/index.html**

Licensing Fees: $700

Additional Information: A state exam is required. A surety bond and a net worth of at least $50,000 are required. The broker must maintain a physical office in New Jersey.

New Mexico

Financial Institutions Division
2550 Cerrillos Road, 3rd Floor
Santa Fe, NM 87505
Phone: 505-476-4885
Web site: **www.rld.state.nm.us/FID/index.html**

Licensing Fees: $400

Additional Information: A surety bond is required.

New York

New York State Banking Department
Mortgage Banking Division
One State Street
New York, NY 10004-1417
Phone: 877-226-5697
Web site: **www.banking.state.ny.us/iambla.htm**

Licensing Fees: $500 and $99 fingerprint fee

Additional Information: Three business references, a background investigation, a personal credit report, and a surety bond are required. Two years of mortgage experience must be verified prior to licensing.

North Carolina

North Carolina Commissioner of Banks
4309 Mail Service Center
Raleigh, NC 27699-4309
Phone: 919-733-3016
Web site: **www.nccob.org/NCCOB/Mortgage**

Licensing Fees: $1,000 and $49 background investigation fee

Additional Information: A background investigation, a personal credit report, and three years of previous experience in mortgage lending are required. Applicants must complete a course in North Carolina Mortgage Fundamentals, and pass the state exam. Brokers must maintain a physical office in the state of North Carolina.

North Dakota

North Dakota Department of Financial Institutions
2000 Schafer Street, Suite G
Bismarck, ND 58501-1204
Phone: 701-328-9933
Web site: **www.nd.gov/dfi**

Licensing Fees: $300 licensing fee and $400 background investigation fee

Additional Information: The broker's license in North Dakota is called a Money Broker. A surety bond is required.

Ohio

Ohio Department of Commerce
Division of Financial Institutions
77 South High Street, 21st Floor
Columbus, OH 43215-6120
Phone: 614-728-8400
Web site: **www.com.state.oh.us/dfi/MortgageBrokers.aspx**

Licensing Fees: $350

Additional Information: Three years of experience in the mortgage lending industry, a surety bond, background investigation, and an exam are required.

Oklahoma

Oklahoma Department of Consumer Credit
4545 North Lincoln Boulevard, Suite 104
Oklahoma City, OK 73105-3408
Phone: 405-521-3653
Web site: **www.okdocc.state.ok.us/mainMB.php**

Licensing Fees: $750 licensing fee and $150 test fee

Additional Information: Three years of experience in the mortgage or lending industry, an exam, and a trust account in a federally insured Oklahoma bank are required. Broker must maintain a physical office in the state.

Oregon

Division of Finance & Corporate Securities
PO Box 14480
Salem, OR 97309-0405
Phone: 866-814-9710
Web site: **http://dfcs.oregon.gov/mortgage_lending.html**

Licensing Fees: $850

Additional Information: Applicants must have three years of experience in the mortgage industry and pass an exam. A surety bond and financial statements are required.

Pennsylvania

Bureau of Licensing and Consumer Compliance
Department of Banking
333 Market Street, 16th Floor
Harrisburg, PA 17101-2290
Phone: 717-878-3717
Web site: **www.banking.state.pa.us/banking/site/default.asp**

Licensing Fees: $500

Additional Information: Applicant must supply detailed work history showing experience in mortgage lending. A background check and fingerprints are required. A license is required for first and second mortgages. Broker must maintain a physical office in the state.

Rhode Island

Department of Business Regulation
233 Richmond Street
Providence, RI 02903
Phone: 401-222-2405
Web site: **www.dbr.ri.gov/divisions/banking_securities/license.php**

Licensing Fees: $550

Additional Information: Applicant must provide work history showing five years of experience in mortgage lending. A background investigation, a surety bond, and a minimum net worth of $10,000 are required.

South Carolina

Department of Consumer Affairs
3600 Forest Drive, 3rd Floor
PO Box 5757
Columbia, SC 29250-5757
Phone: 803-734-4200
Web site: **www.scconsumer.gov/licensing/mortgage_brokers.htm**

Licensing Fees: $750

Additional Information: Applicants must have two years of experience working under a licensed broker. A surety bond is required.

South Dakota

Division of Banking
217 ½ West Missouri Avenue
Pierre, SD 57501
Phone: 605-773-3421
Web site: **www.state.sd.us/drr2/reg/bank/licensees/mortgagebrokers.htm**

Licensing Fees: $365

Additional Information: A background check and a surety bond are required.

Tennessee

Department of Financial Institutions
Nashville City Center
511 Union Street, Suite 400
Nashville, TN 37219
Phone: 615-741-2236
Web site: **www.tennessee.gov/tdfi**

Licensing Fees: $600

Additional Information: A surety bond, audited financial statements, and a minimum net worth of $25,000 are required.

Texas

Texas Department of Savings & Mortgage Lending
Attn: Division of Licensing
2601 North Lamar, Suite 201
Austin, TX 78705
Phone: 512-475-1350 select option 2 for licensing
Web site: **www.sml.state.tx.us/mblolicensing.htm**

Licensing Fees: $434

Additional Information: A written exam, a background investigation, and financial statements are required. A surety bond or a net worth of $25,000 are required.

Utah

Division of Real Estate
PO Box 146711
Salt Lake City, UT 84114-6711
Phone: 801-530-6747
Web site: **http://dopl.utah.gov**

Licensing Fees: $275

Additional Information: Three years of prior experience and 40 hours instruction at a certified premortgage licensing school and a state exam are required. Background investigation including fingerprinting is required.

Vermont

Department of Banking, Insurance, Securities and Health Care Administration
89 Main Street, Drawer 20
Montpelier, VT 05620
Phone: 802-828-3307
Web site: **www.bishca.state.vt.us/BankingDiv/lenderapplic/licensee_applic-reports_index_main.htm**

Licensing Fees: $350 licensing fee and $250 investigation fee

Additional Information: A surety bond and financial statements are required.

Virginia

Bureau of Financial Institutions
1300 E Main Street, Suite 800
PO Box 640
Richmond, VA 23218-0640
Phone: 804-371-9690
Web site: **www.scc.virginia.gov/bfi/applic/mort.aspx**

Licensing Fees: $500

Additional Information: A surety bond, financial statements, and annual financial reports are required.

Washington

Washington State Department of Financial Institutions
Division of Consumer Services
PO Box 41200
Olympia, WA 98504
Phone: 360-902-8700
Web site: **www.dfi.wa.gov/cs/mortgage_licensing.htm**

Licensing Fees: $371

Additional Information: A licensing seminar class, an exam, and a surety bond are all required.

Washington, District of Columbia

Department of Banking and Financial Institutions
1400 I Street NW, Suite 400
Washington, DC 20005
Phone: 202-727-1563
Web site: **www.dbfi.dc.gov**

Licensing Fees: $1,100

Additional Requirements: A minimum net worth of $10,000 and a surety bond are required.

West Virginia

West Virginia Division of Banking
1900 Kanawha Boulevard East, Building 3, Room 311
Charleston, WV 25305-0240
Phone: 304-558-2294
Web site: **www.wvdob.org/professionals/n_mortgage.htm**

Licensing Fees: $350

Additional Information: A surety bond, financial statements, background investigation with fingerprints, a minimum net worth of $10,000, and a FICO score greater than 575 on the personal credit report are all required.

Wisconsin

Department of Financial Institutions
Division of Banking
PO Box 7876
Madison, WI 53707-7876
Phone: 608-261-9555
Web site: **www.wdfi.org/fi/mortbank/babr.htm**

Licensing Fees: $750

Additional Information: A surety bond, background investigation, and exam are required. The broker must maintain a physical office in the state of Wisconsin.

Wyoming

Department of Audit Division of Banking
Herschler Building
3rd Floor East
122 W 25th Street
Cheyenne, WY 82002
Phone: 307-777-7797
Web site: **http://audit.state.wy.us/banking**

Licensing Fees: $500

Additional Information: A surety bond and an exam are required.

Bibliography

Comtois, James. "Calyx Software Market Leader in Loan Origination Systems." Available online at **www.brokeruniverse.com/technology/2007-09-05/comtois.html.**

Cox, Jerry. Personal interview.

Cox, John. "Software Applications Case Studies: Mortgage Broker Banks on Smart Phones." *Network World*, July 3, 2006. Available online at **http://www.techworld.com/applications/features/index.cfm?featureid=2646.**

Crawford, Darryl. Personal interview.

Deis, Karen. "RESPA Cracking Down on Kickbacks and Referral Gifts." *Loan Officer Magazine*, April 2004. Available online at **www.loanofficermagazine.com/archives/archives_action2.php?article_number=176.**

Der Hovanesian, Mara. "Nightmare Mortgages." *Business Week*, September 11, 2006. Available online at **www.businessweek.com/magazine/content/06_37/b4000001.htm.**

Harney, Kenneth. "Study Shows Loan Brokers' Better Side." *The Washington Post*, April 16, 2005, Page F01.

Hechinger, John. "Mortgage Brokers Benefit From a Refinancing Boom." *The Wall Street Journal* Online. Available online at **www.collegejournal.com/salarydata/banking/20030304-hechinger.html.**

Hoppough, Suzanne. "The New Unions." *Forbes*, February 25, 2008. Available online at **www.forbes.com/forbes/2008/0225/100.html.**

"Business Plan Building, Section by Section." *Inc.* magazine. Available online at **www.inc.com/guides/write_biz_plan/20660.html.**

Internal Revenue Service. "Home Office Deduction." Available online at **www.irs.gov/newsroom/article/0,,id=108138,00.html.**

Internal Revenue Service. Publication 587, "Business Use of Your Home." Available online at **www.irs.gov/publications/p587/index.html.**

Jackson, Howell E., and Berry, Jeremy. "Kickbacks or Compensation: The Case of Yield Spread Premiums." Harvard Law School. Available online at **www.law.harvard.edu/faculty/hjackson/pdfs/january_draft.pdf.**

Kahn, Daniel S., and Borden, Marian Edleman. *Success as a Mortgage Broker*. Indianapolis, IN: Alpha Books, 2006.

Kamadia, Ameen. *Jump Start Your Mortgage Career*. Houston: Kamrock Publishing, 2007.

Kamadia, Ameen. *So You Want to Be a Mortgage Broker*. Houston: Kamrock Publishing, 2005.

Lambert, Ken. Personal interview.

Myer, Warren. "The Internet's Adoption Curve." *Mortgage Broker Magazine,* October 2003. Available online at **www.myers.com/press/articles/1003.html.**

Paul, Alex. "Broker: Loan Legislation Could Hurt Consumers." *Albany Democrat Herald,* May 31, 2007. Available online at **www.gazettetimes.com/articles/2007/05/31/news/community/3loc08_loanlegislation.txt.**

Perkins, Broderick. "Was Your Yield Spread Premium Disclosed?" *Realty Times.* Available online at **www.realtytimes.com/rtpages/20020130_yield.htm.**

Pearce, James, and Miller, James. "Freddie Mac and Fannie Mae: Their Funding Advantage & Benefits to Consumers." Congressional Budget Office Report, January 2001 Available online at **www.freddiemac.com/corporate/about/policy/pdf/cbo-final-pearcemiller%5B1%5D.pdf.**

Rebchook, John. "Mortgage Broker Crackdown." *Rocky Mountain News.* March 20, 2008.

Reed, David. *Your Successful Career as a Mortgage Broker.* New York: Amacom Books, 2007.

Rhodes, Elizabeth. "Mortgage Brokers Tighten Rules on Loan Officers." *The Seattle Times,* January 6, 2007. Available online at: **http://seattletimes.nwsource.com/html/realestate/2003511679_mortgage07.html.**

Samuel, Duncan. "How Conveyancing Can Provide an Additional Income Stream for Brokers." *Mortgage Introducer* magazine, May

14, 2007. Available online at **www.convex.net/company_info/press_release_display.jsp?display_id=4213.**

Schlicke, Jillayne. "Mortgage Fraud Case Studies." *Rain City Guide*, November 30, 2007. Available online at **www.raincityguide.com/2007/11/30/mortgage-fraud-case-studies.**

Singletary, Michelle. "Some Mortgage Originators Skip State Licensing." *The Washington Post*. Sunday, September 9, 2007, Page F01.

Small Business Administration. "Manage Your Business from Start to Finish." Available online at **www.sba.gov/smallbusinessplanner/index.html.**

Small Business Administration. "Small Business Size Standards." Available online at **www.sba.gov/services/contractingopportunities/sizestandardstopics/index.html.**

U.S. Department of Housing and Urban Development. "More Information on RESPA (Real Estate Settlement Procedures Act)." Available at **www.hud.gov/offices/hsg/sfh/res/respamor.cfm.**

U.S. Department of Housing and Urban Development. "Statements of Policy Regarding Lender Payments to Mortgage Brokers." Available online at **www.hud.gov/offices/hsg/sfh/res/respapol.cfm.**

U.S. Department of Labor, Bureau of Statistics. "Occupational Outlook Handbook" Available online at **www.bls.gov/oco.**

U.S. Law. "Truth in Lending Act: Protect Your Credit Report." Available online at **www.uslaw.com/library/article/bbktilact.html?area_id=11.**

Wilson, Lloyd. "A Taxonomic Analysis of Mortgage Broker Licensing Statues: Developing a Programmatic Response to Predatory Lending." *New Mexico Law Review*, Volume 36, No. 2, Spring 2006. Available online at **http://lawschool.unm.edu/nmlr/volumes/36/vol2.php.**

TOWNHOUSE
FOR
SALE
Exclusive Agent:

Glossary

A credit: A term used to denote excellent credit for a borrower.

Acceleration clause: A clause in a mortgage agreement that allows the lender to accelerate the loan and demand payment of the outstanding balance. This is generally tied to the failure to make regular payments or becoming delinquent in property taxes.

Adjustable-rate mortgage: A type of mortgage where the interest rate fluctuates according to a rate index. Initially, these loans often have a lower teaser rate, which will increase after the initial period of the loan. After this time, the rate fluctuates periodically for the life of the loan.

Adjustment interval: The period of time between changes in interest rate for an adjustable-rate mortgage. This is the period of time when the payment stays the same before the rate and payment will change. The interval varies among ARMs.

Alternative documentation: This is sometimes referred to as limited doc, which means less documentation is needed to secure a loan. The good thing about these loans is that the time for approval is generally less. The borrower will need to have excellent or very good credit and meet income requirements for the past two years to qualify for these loans.

Amortization: The gradual reduction in the principal over time is known as amortization. Over the life of the loan, the borrower makes monthly payments. An amortization schedule shows the money being applied to principal and interest from each payment. If the loan is paid in regular monthly payments, as with a fixed-rate mortgage, the balance will be paid off at the end of the term.

Amortization schedule: A table used by the lender which shows the amount of the payment that is applied to principal and interest each month over the term of the loan.

Annual Percentage Rate (APR): The actual interest rate of the loan when closing costs and points are calculated.

Application: The application required to borrow money for a home loan.

Application fee: Money charged to the borrower at the time of the application. This is generally a flat fee which is meant to cover the lender's cost for processing the application. It is often included in the closing costs.

Appraisal: An expert valuation of the market value of a particular property. A professional appraiser will inspect the property and use recently sold comparable properties to determine the value of a property. This is needed for all mortgages, second mortgages, and refinance loans.

Appraisal fee: The fee charged by an appraiser for doing the appraisal on a property. This fee can vary, but is often between $300 and $400.

Assumable mortgage: Some mortgages can be assumed by the new owner when the home is sold.

Automated underwriting: This is a system where mortgage approvals are automatically generated by computer. The borrower's income, credit history, and other data are used to generate the decision. Information is verified after the approval.

Bad credit loans: Loans made to borrowers with poor credit. The interest rate is generally higher than for borrowers with good credit.

Balloon mortgage: Similar to a fixed-rate mortgage, but the loan is not amortized. The full amount of the loan will come due when the loan matures. At this time, the borrower must either pay off the loan, sell, or refinance. The rate is generally lower on balloon loans.

Bankruptcy: A court proceeding during which an individual or business is offered relief from debts the person or business cannot pay. Chapter 7 bankruptcy is known as liquidation and the debtor's assets are sold to pay creditors. Chapter 11 bankruptcy is used for reorganization of businesses and the owner continues to operate the business while repaying creditors on a schedule approved by the court. Chapter 13 is a repayment plan in which an individual agrees to make partial payments over a three- to five-year period. This requires the individual to file a budget with the court.

Bridge loan: A short-term loan which provides temporary financing for a home purchase until the borrower is able to secure permanent financing for the purchase. The property is used to secure the loan as in a traditional mortgage.

Buy down: A situation in which the lender lowers the interest rate in exchange for the borrower paying points. The borrower is basically buying a lower interest rate with the money paid in points.

Buyer's expenses: The expenses paid by the borrower for the purchase of a property. These include fees for document stamps, recording the deed, attorney's fees, appraisals, inspection, surveys, title insurance, and escrow fees.

Cash out: The borrower draws cash out of the home when refinancing the mortgage. The amount of cash a borrower can take depends on several factors including the value of the home, amount of the mortgage, income, and credit. The borrower receives this money in a check after closing.

Clear title: After the title search, a property is found to be clear of any liens or other encumbrances.

Closing costs: Fees paid by the buyer or seller at closing. Closing costs include fees for surveys, inspection, recording, appraisals, and professional fees for brokers and attorneys. Fees charged by the title company, points paid on the loan, and homeowner's insurance are some of the other fees that may be charged at closing.

Collateral: Items of value used to secure a loan. Using collateral gives the lender security in the event the borrower defaults on the loan. For the purposes of a mortgage, the collateral used is the property.

Commitment letter: A letter from the lender promising a mortgage at a specific interest rate.

Comparable sales: These are used in determining the appraised value of a property. The selling prices of homes of a comparable size in the same area are used to determine the market value of the property being mortgaged.

Conforming loan: A loan that conforms to the requirements of Freddie Mac and Fannie Mae is a conforming loan.

Construction financing: A short-term loan taken for the construction of a home. When construction is completed, the borrower takes a traditional mortgage to purchase the home. Construction financing is generally taken by the builder or developer, rather than the homeowner. When the mortgage is secured, this loan is paid off.

Consumer Price Index (CPI): An economic indicator used to track the costs of goods and services. The CPI is an indicator of inflation. Surveys are taken each month to determine the CPI.

Conventional loan: A fixed-rate, 30-year mortgage that is not secured by the federal government.

Credit bureau: A company that creates and maintains the credit reports of people in the United States. There are three major credit reporting bureaus: Equifax, Trans Union, and Experian. Creditors report information on borrowers to the bureau. This information is used to create a credit report.

Credit report: A report showing a borrower's credit history for paying bills. The report shows payment history for loans and other accounts as well as any delinquencies or negative information regarding the payment history.

Debt consolidation: When a borrower takes a loan against property and uses the money to pay off other debts, such as loans and credit cards. The borrower's debts are consolidated into one payment, generally with a lower interest rate.

Debt-to-income ratio: The debt-to-income ratio is calculated by dividing your total monthly payments by the total monthly income. This formula is used by lenders to determine if a borrower can afford to make the monthly payments on a loan. The percentage required varies according to the type of loan, but most hover around a maximum in the range of 40 percent.

Deed: A legal document for the transfer of real property from one party (the seller) to another party (the buyer).

Default: When a borrower falls behind in monthly mortgage payments. If the payments are 90 days or more past due, the lender considers the loan to be in default. This puts the borrower at risk of foreclosure.

Delinquent: When a borrower falls behind in payments, the account is said to be delinquent.

Discount points: Money paid by the borrower at closing in exchange for a lower interest rate on a mortgage. One point is equal to one percent of the total amount financed.

Discount rate: The interest rate the Federal Reserve charges for loaning money to commercial banks.

Down payment: The amount of money the borrower must put down to secure a home loan. This can vary from 5 to 25 percent.

Earnest money: A deposit given by the buyer to the seller when an agreement is reached for the sale of a property. This deposit shows that the buyer is serious about purchasing the property. In general, the money is not refundable if the buyer changes his mind unless the reason is an inability to secure financing for the purchase.

Errors and omissions insurance: This type of liability insurance covers the mortgage broker against errors or mistakes in business. This policy only covers honest errors, not fraudulent actions on the part of the broker.

Escrow: Funds held in an escrow account until a specific event or date. The money is then released to the appropriate entity, organization, or individual. For home mortgages, escrow accounts are often used to pay property taxes and homeowner's insurance premiums.

Equity: The difference between the current market value of the home and the amount owed. If the home is worth $200,000 and the borrower owes $125,000 on a mortgage, the equity is $75,000.

Fannie Mae: Fannie Mae is the nickname for the Federal National Mortgage Association. This is a government-sponsored, publicly owned corporation. Fannie Mae is the largest source of funding for mortgages in the United States.

Fee-based income: The income of the mortgage broker based on fees, such as loan origination fees.

Federal Housing Administration (FHA): The FHA administers loans. These loans generally come with higher insurance premiums and a maximum loan amount, which is based on the average housing costs in a specific area.

Federal Reserve: The system of federal banks which regulates the money supply in the United States. The Fed regulates the money supply by setting the discount rate of interest and buying and selling securities. The Fed attempts to prevent inflation by taking a variety of measures such as raising the discount interest rate and decreasing the money supply in the country.

FICO score: The FICO score is a credit score. These are used by mortgage lenders to predict the borrower's ability and willingness to pay debts. FICO is an acronym for the Fair Isaac Corporation, which calculates the credit scores in the United States.

Final inspection: The last inspection of the property being purchased prior to closing. This inspection is done to determine the condition of the property and ensure the property is in the same condition as at the time of the agreement of sale.

Fixed-rate mortgage: A mortgage where the interest rate remains the same for the life of the loan. This results in fixed monthly payments.

Float: When the borrower has been approved for a mortgage but is waiting for paperwork to be completed and closing scheduled, the borrower may chose to either float or lock the interest rate. Floating the rate means the borrower is waiting to see if the rate will go lower in the interim. Since rates are always fluctuating, there is a chance the rate could either increase or decrease prior to closing.

Foreclosure: A court proceeding which occurs when a borrower fails to pay the mortgage. The owner loses his rights to the home, which the lender then sells to pay off the debt.

Freddie Mac: A nickname for the Federal Home Loan Mortgage Corporation. Along with Fannie Mae, Freddie Mac purchases qualifying mortgages from lenders and sells them as mortgage-backed securities. Freddie Mac was created to bring stability to the mortgage market in the U.S.

Full-doc loan: A mortgage loan that requires verification of all the income, assets, and other financial information of the borrower.

Fully amortizing payments: A payment structure where the monthly payment is enough to pay off the principal and interest on a loan by the end of the term. Fixed-rate mortgages are generally fully amortizing.

Ginnie Mae: Ginnie Mae is a government corporation under the United States Department of Housing and Urban Development (HUD). Mortgages secured by Ginnie Mae are usually FHA loans. These loans are typically given to low-income and first-time homeowners. Ginnie Mae does not issue or purchase mortgages, but guarantees loans.

Good Faith Estimate: A written disclosure which must be given to the borrower by the lender and the mortgage broker. The Good Faith Estimate contains a list of estimated closing costs and other fees for the purchase of a home. This statement is required by law.

Graduated-payment mortgage: This type of mortgage has monthly payments that start out low and gradually increase every year. The amount of increase is fixed, unlike ARMs. This loan has lower monthly payments in the early years. Negative amortization can happen, especially if home values fall.

Hazard insurance: A type of insurance which offers protection against hazards such as fire, storm, and vandalism. This is generally required by lenders as a condition of the mortgage. The insurance protects against loss if a hazard were to occur at the property.

Home equity line of credit: A type of second mortgage where money is taken in draws, rather than in one lump sum. Lines of credit are often used to pay for education and home repairs or improvement projects. Money can be borrowed up to the maximum amount of the line of credit.

Home improvement loan: A mortgage to finance an addition or renovation of a home.

Homeowner's insurance: This is an insurance policy which provides protection against damage to the home and personal property of the owner. Homeowner's policies cover a wide variety of events including fire, storm damage, vandalism, burglary, and other incidents which cause damage to property. Policies also contain some personal liability coverage to protect against lawsuits resulting from injury to another person on your property. The coverage in these plans is much more comprehensive than hazard insurance.

HUD or the U.S. Department of Housing and Urban Development: This entity insures mortgage loans for low-income home buyers. HUD also sets minimum standards for the properties eligible for HUD insured loans.

Index: A measure of economic conditions used to calculate monthly payments. A predetermined margin is added to the index figure to calculate the interest on adjustable-rate mortgages. A few different indexes are used by lenders to make these calculations.

Inspection: Inspection is done prior to the purchase of a home to ensure the house is in good condition without major damage or structural flaws. In some cases, the lender will require an inspection for financing. This is always required for FHA loans. The buyer has the right to hire a private inspector prior to purchasing the property. In most cases, the agreement of sale is contingent upon passing the inspection.

Installment loan: A type of loan where borrowed money is repaid in payments made at regular intervals for a specific period of time.

Interest-only mortgage: Payments are made only on the interest of the loan for a fixed term, usually in the beginning of the term. The unpaid principal balance is either paid in monthly installments after the initial period or in a balloon payment at the end of the term.

Interest rate: The schedule of money charged by a lender for borrowing monthly. The rate is calculated annually and is a percentage of the total amount borrowed for the mortgage.

Interest rate cap: This is a provision in adjustable-rate mortgages which limits the amount the interest rate can increase. There are periodic interest rate caps which limit increases during each adjustment period. Most loans also have lifetime caps. This is a limit on how many percentage points the interest rate can increase over the life of the loan.

Jumbo loan: A mortgage that is above the maximum amount allowed by Fannie Mae or Freddie Mac. This maximum changes according to average housing costs.

Leads: Leads are prospective clients who are in the market for a home loan and interested in working with a mortgage broker. There are a variety of ways to get leads. Once the mortgage broker receives a lead about a prospective client, he needs to contact the client and sell his brokerage services. Mortgage brokers are continually cultivating leads to generate new business.

Lead generation: Lead generation uses technology to generate new leads for the mortgage broker. This can be done through the use of a database or a computer program. Online lead-generation services promise a large number of leads for a price. Some of these companies offer a good service, but others only sell lists of names and tend to sell these lists to more than one broker. Do some research if using a lead-generation company to be sure you are getting what you are paying for.

Lender policy: This is a title insurance policy that covers the lender against loss related to liens or other encumbrances on the title to a property.

Liability insurance: This is an insurance policy which offers the policyholder protection against lawsuits. For mortgage brokers, this would cover claims that the broker was negligent or failed to fulfill his duties to the client or the lender.

Lien: A legal claim against a property or asset to secure a loan. The lien gives the lien holder an interest in the property in the event of a default on the loan. In the case of a mortgage, home equity loan, second mortgage, or line of credit, the lender has a lien against the property. The first lien holder is the lender for the primary mortgage. If the borrower takes out a second mortgage, this lender is in second position behind the primary lender in the event of a loss or default.

Loan: A financial agreement in which one party (the lender) gives money to another party (the borrower). In exchange for the loan, the borrower agrees to pay the lender monthly payments based on the amount of the loan plus interest.

Loan-to-value ratio (LTV): The amount of the total mortgage divided by the value of the property. Lenders have guidelines and limits for LTV and higher ratios often require the buyer to obtain mortgage insurance.

Loan officer: A representative of the lender also called a loan representative or account executive. A loan officer is employed by the lender and acts on behalf of the lender.

Loan origination fee: A fee which is charged by the lender for processing a loan application. The fee is stated as a percentage of the total amount of the loan.

Loan processor: A loan processor completes several tasks on behalf of the lender. Mortgage brokers sometimes employ loan processors to handle some of the paperwork on behalf of the broker. The processor takes the application, checks the credit, arranges for appraisals, and generally assists the broker or lender in the process.

Lock: The process which allows a borrower to lock the interest rate on a loan. Once the rate is locked, it will not change if interest rates increase or decrease while the borrower is waiting to go to closing.

Margin: The margin is the difference between the index and the interest rate charged on an adjustable-rate mortgage. The margin is determined at closing and is defined as the number of percentage points added to the index to calculate the interest rate for an ARM. The margin is the same over the term of the loan. When the interest rate changes, it is due to a change in the index rather than the margin.

Market value: The amount of money a home is worth based on the selling price of other homes of the same size in the same general location. This is the amount of money the house can bring on the open market.

Mortgage: A mortgage is an agreement for a loan to purchase property. The property is used as collateral in the event the borrower defaults on the loan. The interest rate and monthly payment schedule are spelled out in the agreement. The borrower signs a promissory note for the debt.

Mortgage calculator: A tool or program used to determine the monthly payment on a mortgage. These calculators use the amount financed, term of the loan and interest rate to calculate the monthly payment.

Mortgagee: The entity lending the money in a mortgage transaction. This is also called the lender or mortgage company.

Mortgage-backed securities: These are securities sold on the stock market which are backed by the principal and interest payments on a pool of mortgage loans. A large number of mortgages are bundled together and sold as mortgage-backed securities. This generates more money for future mortgage lending. These are residential mortgage loans. There are also commercial mortgage-backed securities which are secured by commercial or multifamily properties.

Mortgage broker: A professional who helps borrowers connect with lenders who have loan programs to meet the needs of the borrower.

Brokers also advise clients when selecting loans and handle the application process, but they do not grant loans.

Mortgage insurance: Insurance that lenders require borrowers to purchase when the down payment is less than 20 percent of the value of the property. This insurance protects the lender against loss.

Mortgage lender: A company that lends money to borrowers for the purchase of homes.

Mortgage term: The amount of time in which the borrower must repay the mortgage loan. This is generally 15 or 30 years, depending on the loan.

Mortgagor: The person or persons borrowing money in a mortgage transaction. This person is also known as the borrower or buyer.

Negative amortization: A normal fixed-rate mortgage has an amortization schedule that will result in the principal and interest being paid off by the end of the term. The gradual reduction in the principal over time is known as amortization. When the principal is not being paid down, as with some ARMs and interest-only loans, the loan does not fully amortize by the end of the term. The unpaid portions of interest or principal are then added to the end of the loan, which makes the balance increase.

Negative amortization cap: This is the limit of negative amortization that is allowed on an adjustable-rate mortgage. The cap is expressed as a percentage of the total amount of the loan.

Niche market: A term used to describe a specialized segment of a particular market. For example, in the mortgage brokerage business, a niche market would be a specific group of potential borrowers with which a broker specializes. Examples of niche markets include police officers, teachers, and self employed individuals.

No-doc loan: In this type of mortgage loan, the borrower does not have to have income verified or even state his income. Only borrowers with excellent credit will qualify for this type of mortgage.

Nonconforming loans: Loans which do not meet the standards and requirements of Freddie Mac and Fannie Mae. This could be the result of the size of the loan, credit score of the borrower, verification of income, and many other factors. Basically, all loans which do not conform to Freddie Mac and Fannie Mae are considered nonconforming loans.

Owner's policy: In title insurance, this is the part of the policy that protects the borrower in the event something were to go wrong with the title, such as a lien that was missed in the title search. This policy is designed to protect the borrower against losses of this type.

Payment cap: A payment cap is a maximum amount of money the monthly payment on a mortgage may increase in a period of time. There are periodic caps on adjustable-rate mortgages that limit the amount of money the monthly payment can increase from one adjustment period to the next. Most loans also have a lifetime cap which limits the total amount the monthly payment can increase over the term of the loan.

Piggyback mortgage: A second mortgage that is taken at the same time as the first mortgage and closes at the same time. This is a smaller amount which is typically between 10 and 20 percent of the total amount financed under both loans. Piggyback mortgages are sometimes used in place of jumbo loans to avoid the higher interest rate on the total amount of money financed.

PITI: An acronym which stands for principal, interest, taxes, and insurance. These figures are used to calculate the total monthly payment.

Private mortgage insurance (PMI): This is insurance required by lenders when the borrower finances over 80 percent of the value of the property. This insurance is intended to protect the lender in the event of a default on the part of the borrower. The cost of this insurance is about one half of 1 percent of the total loan amount. Once the equity in the home increases to more than 20 percent of the value, the PMI is no longer required, in most cases.

Points: One point is equal to 1 percent of the total amount financed. Borrowers can sometimes pay points in exchange for a slightly lower interest rate.

Preapproval: A buyer with good credit can get preapproved before shopping for a home. The lender checks the borrower's credit and income to determine how much they can borrow. This gives the borrower a price range for home shopping, but is not a guarantee for a loan.

Prepaid interest: Interest collected at the time of closing for the balance of the month. This is a partial month's interest payment for the remainder of the current month in which closing takes place.

Prepaid items: These are other costs paid at closing in addition to interest. These items can include payments for taxes and insurance, which may be required by the lender.

Prepayment penalty: A fee charged by lenders if the borrower pays off the loan during the penalty period. These are often seen with subprime mortgages. The penalty phase is generally stated in years, usually from one to three. If the borrower pays off the loan before that time, there will be a penalty. This can vary but is often expressed as a certain number of months' interest.

Prequalification: A more detailed process where the borrower provides enough financial information to secure a commitment from the lender. This process determines how much money a buyer can borrow for a mortgage. Buyers should get at least two or three lenders for prequalification.

Principal: This is the amount of money borrowed for the purchase of a home. As payments are made, the principal is gradually lowered over the term of the loan.

Realtor: A real estate broker or agent who is affiliated with the National Association of Realtors.

Real Estate Settlement Procedures Act (RESPA): A federal law which regulates the settlement procedures in the real estate industry. Some of the provisions of RESPA include providing the client with a Good Faith Estimate of the closing costs that will be incurred. This law also prohibits kickbacks for referrals for services related to real estate. Paying a Realtor for leads would be considered a kickback by the mortgage broker and would be a violation of this law.

Refinance: A new mortgage which will be used to pay off an existing loan. This is generally done to secure a lower rate or a fixed-rate mortgage.

Reverse mortgage: A type of tax-free home mortgage through which owners can borrow against the equity in the home with no payments. At the term of the loan, the principal and interest is due in one balloon payment. Older people often use reverse mortgages to cover a variety of expenses. The mortgage comes due upon the death of the homeowner.

Right of rescission: The legal right of a borrower to change his mind about a loan within three days of closing. This is a provision of the Truth in Lending Act. If the borrower is taking cash out at closing on a refinance loan or consolidating debts, no monies are released until after the right of rescission period has passed.

Sales contract: A written agreement between the buyer and seller which states the terms of the sale of a piece of property.

Secondary mortgage market: The financial market where existing mortgages are packaged and sold as mortgage-backed securities. The secondary mortgage market is a major source of funding for mortgage lending.

Second mortgage: A type of home equity loan through which a homeowner borrows money against the equity in the home. The lender for the second mortgage is in second position behind the primary lender to collect money in the event the property would be sold in foreclosure.

Seller: In a real estate agreement, this is the person selling his or her home.

Seller's expenses: The costs paid by the seller at closing in a real estate transaction. These fees include document stamps, real estate commissions, attorney's fees, surveys, cost of abstract, and escrow fees.

Settlement statement: A statement given to borrowers at closing. This statement discloses all costs and fees associated with the purchase of the home. The total amount of interest paid over the life of the loan, closing costs, origination fees, and all other costs are spelled out in this statement.

Subprime lender: A lender who gives mortgages to borrowers with poor credit who do not meet the criteria for a conforming or conventional mortgage. These lenders charge higher fees and interest rates in exchange for taking on the additional risk that is associated with subprime loans.

Subprime mortgage market: Subprime lenders make loans to borrowers with poor credit. These lenders charge an interest rate that can be significantly higher than the prime rate.

Survey: A professional measurement of land involved in real estate transactions. The survey shows the exact location of the land including boundaries and reference points. The size, location, and dimensions of the property are included in the survey.

Teaser rate: The lower introductory rate offered on adjustable-rate mortgages. The introductory rate on these loans is typically lower than the rate on a comparable fixed-rate mortgage. The borrower enjoys the lower teaser rate for the first one to five years, depending on the loan. After this initial period, the loan converts to an ARM and payments can increase or decrease with interest rates.

Title: A legal document showing an individual's right to ownership in a specific property. This is also known as the title deed and shows the history of ownership and transfer of title from one owner to the next since the construction of the home until the present time.

Title company: This company performs the title search on the property and prepares all the necessary documents required for closing on a mortgage. Closing often takes place in the offices of the title company.

Title search: A search performed on the title or deed of a property. The search looks for liens or other encumbrances that would interfere with the transfer of the title from one party to the other in a real estate transaction. Any liens or judgments must be cleared for the title to be considered clear.

Title insurance: A policy purchased to protect against loss caused by issues with the title, such as missed liens or other similar issues. The policy may cover the lender, borrower, or both. In many cases, the borrower is required to pay title insurance to cover both himself and the lender.

Truth in Lending: A federal law requiring the disclosure of certain information to borrowers involved in loan transactions and entering into loan agreements. This is meant to help consumers compare terms between companies. Things like prepayment penalties, interest rates, and associated loan costs must be included on the Truth in Lending statement.

Underwriter: A representative of the mortgage lender. The underwriter approves the loan package and provides the money for the purchase.

Uniform Settlement Statement: The standard HUD form used for disclosure of costs at settlement. This statement includes all charges and fees associated with the purchase of the home.

Verification of deposit: A form that is used to verify that the borrower has a specific sum of money deposited at a bank or other financial institution.

Verification of employment: A form that verifies and documents the employment history of the borrower and coborrower. The past two years are the most important to the lender.

Veterans Affairs (VA): The VA administers loans for veterans of the U.S. military. There are specific guidelines to qualify for VA loans.

Wholesale lender: These lenders have funds to lend and use mortgage brokers to secure loans for them. Some large lenders have both a wholesale division that works with brokers and a retail division that offers loans to the general public. Wholesale lenders generally have lower interest rates.

Yield spread premium (YSP): A fee paid by a lender to the mortgage broker in exchange for a higher interest rate. The YSP covers the broker's fee, but gives the client a slightly higher interest rate. The YSP is expressed in points with one point being equal to one percent of the total amount financed in the mortgage.

Index

M

N

P

R

S

T

U

W

Made in the USA
Middletown, DE
27 January 2021

32575599R00159